Twentieth Century

CHECKERS

GROVER—WISWELL BOOKS

Twentieth Century Checkers

Let's Play Checkers

Checker Magic

Checkers

Chess

Left to right: JESSE B. HANSON; Sheriff LEE CROFT, Hanson's second; TOMMIE WISWELL, Grover's second; JAMES A. BUSH, Chairman of Match Committee; KENNETH M. GROVER

Twentieth Century

CHECKERS

By

KENNETH M. GROVER

Pacific Coast Champion, U. S. Eleven
Man Ballot Champion, Runner-up Tenth
American Tourney

and

TOMMIE WISWELL

United States Number One Problemist,
former U. S. Army and New York
Champion

FEATURING THE
GROVER-HANSON CHAMPIONSHIP GAMES

DAVID McKAY COMPANY

WASHINGTON SQUARE   PHILADELPHIA

DEDICATION

TO THE DAY WHEN ALL OUR BATTLES WILL
BE FOUGHT 'ACROSS THE BOARD' AND THE
ONLY ABSOLUTE MONARCHS WILL BE
CHECKER KINGS

APPRECIATION

The authors wish to thank
LOUIS BURT,
the New York expert, for his
splendid assistance in preparing
the manuscript for publication.

K. M. G. & T. W.

CONTENTS

CONTENTS

Introduction

2 0 T H C E N T U R Y C H E C K E R S

NO DOUBT many readers of this volume are just making
their acquaintance with "three-move restriction" checkers,
which is the style adopted today by all masters and experts in
match and tourney play. For this reason, a few words regarding this style of play may not be amiss.

"Three-move restriction," and even "two-move," for that
matter, has not always been the vogue. As a matter of fact,
both styles of play may truly be termed "20th Century Checkers," especially the former. In the years preceding the turn of
the current century, and long before then, the "Go-as-you-
please" style of play was accepted as standard in the highest
checker circles. It finally became apparent, however, that if
the game was not to become stagnant and suffer from continued repetition of safe lines of play by cautious match
players, innovations would have to be introduced. Masters like
Wyllie, Martins and Barker were playing many important
matches in which the same games were being played over and
over again (with particular emphasis on the "Glasgow," which
is favorable to the first player), as both players when handling
the black pieces would at once open with the "safe" 11–15 and
adhere religiously to the manoeuvres they were familiar with.
Finally, as a last resort to abolish this practice in important
encounters, the "two-move restriction" mode of play was first
officially adopted in 1907, in an American Tourney at Boston.

At this style of play, white's reply to black's opening move, as well as black's initial move, are determined by ballot. Both sides of the same opening must be played by each player, who alternates with the black and white pieces. There are 43 acceptable two-move restriction openings, so that the greater scope and variety afforded by this style of play are at once apparent, in contrast with the now outmoded "Go-as-you-please" style.

It soon became apparent, however, that the average expert with a little spare time could easily "get his lines down" on two-move and still stick pretty close to "P.P." (published play). While much new play was unearthed and many beautiful variations discovered, it became apparent when Sam Gonotsky and Mike Lieber played their famous 40-game match in 1928 that still further restriction was both desired and justified. (This celebrated match between two of the giants of the draughts-board of that period resulted in a deadlock—40 draws! However, Jesse B. Hanson, the Internationalist, who was Lieber's coach for the match, claims Mike missed a win in that famous 8th Game.)

At the Seventh American Tourney in 1929 a committee of experts was appointed to determine the openings to be played under the then new three-move restriction. After considerable discussion and deliberation the committee made its findings public and, as a result, today we have 137 official three-move openings. Under this style of play, black's first *two* moves and white's first move are determined by ballot. While some openings decidedly favor white, all are drawable and in any event both players have a chance at the strong side of each opening.

The first American Tourney officially to adopt the three-move restriction style was the 8th American Championship Congress, held at Jamestown, N. Y. in 1934. Edwin F. Hunt,

of Nashville, Tennessee, was the first three-move champion of America. In 1937 the fraternity found itself split and two national tourneys were held, both at the three-move style. One convened at Providence, Rhode Island, with Nathan Rubin, the celebrated young Detroit star, the ultimate winner, and the other was held in Martins Ferry, Ohio and was won by Asa Long, who needs no introduction to devotees of Damah. The great Asa, who hails from Toledo, Ohio, has since his youth been one of the world's leading masters.

The last three-move tourneys to be held prior to publication of this volume were the Second N. C. A. Tourney in Tacoma, Washington (the locale of this match), won by Willie Ryan, the current World's Champion, and the 10th A.C.A. Tourney, held in Flint, Michigan, in 1939, with Asa Long the winner and Kenneth Grover the runner-up.

The "three-move" or American Restriction, as it is popularly known, is now the accepted mode of play all over North America. We confidently predict it will soon be just as popular, and the standard method of play in Great Britain, and wherever the grand old game is played. It is popular with master and novice alike because of the many new and unexplored lines of play that are developed and because man's native intellectual curiosity will invariably lead him to seek out and triumph over that which eludes and baffles him.

The games which follow are fine examples of this modern method of scientific checker-playing. A close study of them by the reader, with special attention to the appended notes, will help equip him with a sound basis upon which to pursue a further study of "20th Century Checkers."

TOMMIE WISWELL

THE GROVER-HANSON MATCH GAMES

FOR THE
PACIFIC COAST CHAMPIONSHIP
AND A THOUSAND DOLLAR PURSE

KENNETH M. GROVER

New York City

Challenger and Winner

VS.

JESSE B. HANSON

Oakland, Calif.

Defender of Crown

November 4th to December 10th, 1944
Croft Hotel, Tacoma, Washington

THE NUMBERED CHECKER BOARD

It is best to use a numbered board when studying from a book or periodical. There is nothing mystifying or unusual about "playing by the numbers." It is merely the methods the author uses to transmit his thoughts and ideas to the reader. Number your board from 1 to 32, starting at the upper left hand corner, as in the following diagram. The Blacks occupy squares 1 to 12 and the Whites 21 to 32.

"Language of the Checker Board"

BLACK

WHITE

To run up the games in this book move down each column in the game section, then go up to the top of the next right hand column. Although your checker board has the playing squares in Black the diagrams in all books are reversed in order to show up the pieces.

Biographical Sketches of the Contestants

KENNETH M. GROVER

Kenneth Grover was born in Auburn, Indiana May 10th., 1908 but spent a good portion of his younger days in Cleveland, Ohio and Detroit, Michigan, later migrating to New York City. It was in Detroit in 1924 that he received his initiation into the realm of Checker experts. He was fortunate in having such greats of the board as L. T. De Bearn, Nathan Rubin and the late Mike Lieber as his early teachers and sparring partners. Undoubtedly it is this background which is partly responsible for much of Mr. Grover's later successes. It was during these early days of his career that he vied for the Championship of Chess in Michigan and Ohio.

Shortly after the great 7th American Tourney at Cedar Point, Ohio in 1929 where he took one of the minor prizes in a very strong field Grover came to New York. Although the youth did not know it at the time, Gotham town was to be his home for many years to come as well as the scene of many of his great victories. Here he received the necessary "polishing" his game required from the capable hands of Louis Ginsberg and Willie Ryan, two of the greatest players of the present era. Grover has a keen mind and is quick to grasp the finer points of the subject, quickly discarding what is unimportant and as far as he is concerned, unnecessary. With two such great teachers as Ginsberg and Ryan to carry on the work of his Detroit tutors it was not long before "young Grover" (as he has been called for the past 20 years) was attracting nation wide attention. With the advent of three-move Ryan carried on alone and shared all of his secret analytical play with the coming star.

15

One of his first metropolitan victories was a decisive win over Charles Jolly, the greatest player New Jersey ever produced. This match gave Grover confidence and ambition and from then on his string of victories mounted until today he has defeated nearly every outstanding player in America in either match or tourney play. A partial list includes such notables as Asa Long, Willie Ryan, Walter Hallman, Harold Freyer, Louis Ginsberg (the pupil beating the Master), Arthur Reisman, Steve Fairchild, John B. Stiles, Jesse Hanson, Alex Cameron, Monte Schiefer, H. B. Reynolds and Ray Gould.

Besides the Pacific Coast title he holds the United States Eleven Man Ballot Championship. His National Tournament record is indeed an impressive one, stopping just short of the coveted championship. In 1937 he shared third and fourth prizes with Walter Hallman at Martins Ferry, Ohio and two years later was runner-up to Asa Long at Flint, Michigan, where he accomplished his greatest single victory by defeating the Ohio Master in an impressive heat 1–0–3 draws.

Although we are only able to touch on the highlights of Mr. Grover's playing career it is obvious that he easily ranks as one of the Grand Masters of the present day and is a serious contender for the World Championship honors.

Grover has also made an enviable reputation for himself as a writer and teacher of the game. Besides "Twentieth Century Checkers" his numerous books in collaboration with Tommie Wiswell include "Let's Play Checkers" and "Chess." While a recreation leader for the Police League in New York City he wrote "Checkers" a valuable guide for youngsters.

The fact that he is without doubt America's outstanding Checker and Chess exhibition player only demonstrates his amazing versatility. Before World War Two he made several transcontinental tours of this nation and Canada showing his skill at blindfold and simultaneous play. When the war broke

out he (and Tommie Wiswell) joined the Merchant Marine helping transport the vital oil and gasoline up and down the coast, down to the Netherlands West Indies, and numerous trips to the European battlefront.

(Incidentally, Kenneth's brother Willie who served long and faithfully in this branch of the service, after being missing for a year turned up a prisoner of Japan. The latest reports again list him as missing and the War Department lists him as having been on a Japanese ship torpedoed by the Allies.)

An accident temporarily put Kenneth ashore for a spell and later he went to work in the shipyards at Tacoma, Washington. With the world again at peace, Mr. Grover is displaying his talents before many of the Checker Clubs.

Of course the players of Washington were delighted to have such a master in their midst and when Jesse Hanson, John Stiles and other notables started coming to Tacoma it took on the atmosphere of Flint, Michigan in the middle 20's, when most of the greats of the Checker world congregated there during the boom. Since Mr. Hanson had held the Pacific Coast Championship for many years, it was only natural that the match for the title should develop. Lee Croft, Floyd Payne, James A. Bush, Al Flower, Charles I. Pace, Ranson Minkler, Arthur R. Johnson, C. O. Patrick and numerous other Washington promoters got behind the idea and the present volume and match is the result.

JESSE B. HANSON

Jesse B. Hanson was born in Santa Cruz, California on January 24th, 1885. For over a quarter of a century, prior to meeting Mr. Grover, he had been recognized as the Pacific Coast Champion, having defeated all comers with characteristic ease.

Like all Master players he took a liking to the game while

still in his teens and early made a National reputation for himself. He starred as both, a match and tourney player, and in 1927 was honored by being selected to play on the great American team which defeated Great Britain in the Second International match at the Hotel Alamac, in New York City. Jesse acquitted himself nobly in this event and secured for himself, forever, a place in Checkerdom's "Hall of Fame."

His tourney record is a distinguished one, the highlight coming in 1929 when he was runner-up to Samuel Gonotsky at Chicago, where Sammie played in defense of his National Championship. It was in this tourney that Gonotsky played his last great games for shortly thereafter he passed away along with the great Mike Lieber, Hanson's pupil. Gonotsky and Lieber were two of the greatest players America ever produced and in a forty game match they played all draws. Jesse, who coached Mike pointed out a win Lieber missed in one of the games. To Jesse, this will always be the greatest disappointment of his life, although he can well be proud of the fine showing Lieber made against this greatest of all American Champions.

Mr. Hanson has made several world-wide tours, giving displays of his skill and meeting (and defeating) other Champions across the board. His match record is unparalleled, his victims including a goodly number of the famous players of the present era.

Mr. Hanson has a modest and unassuming air and is very popular with the Checker fraternity at large. The fans in this match were divided about 50–50 in their sympathies and those who backed Jesse still have all the confidence in the world in him and would gladly back him in a return match with Mr. Grover. Thus, even in defeat the likable Hanson in-

18

spires confidence and enthusiasm. This is because of his sportsmanlike personality and perseverance.

We believe a return match would be full of interest and anything but a walkover. In fact, Mr. Grover would have his hands full retaining his newly won laurels!

A PARTIAL RECORD OF HANSON'S IMPORTANT MATCHES

1911	*Tied with A. Jordan, London, England*	*10 draws*
1913	*Defeated J. Dougherty,, Los Angeles*	*3–1–17*
1913	*Tied with Fred Hogue, San Francisco*	*2–2–14*
1913	*Defeated J. T. Bradford, Los Angeles*	*3–2–15*
1915	*Lost to J. Drouillard, San Francisco*	*5–4–21*
1918	*Defeated H. Morrall, Boston*	*3–0–17*
1920	*Defeated J. T. Bradford, Cleveland*	*4–1–15*
1922	*Tied with L. M. Lewis, Chicago*	*20 draws*
1924	*Defeated Peter Doran, Seattle*	*3–0–17*
1925	*Defeated Alex Cameron, Cleveland*	*4–1–15*
1927	*Defeated J. Farley, Kansas City, Mo.*	*2–0–14*
1929	*Runner-up to Gonotsky at Chicago*	*2–1–3*
1934	*Lost to E. Hunt, then American Champion*	*5–1–24*
1941	*Defeated Alex Cameron, Hendersonville, N. C.*	*6–3–31*
1944	*Lost to Kenneth Grover, Seattle, Wash.*	*4–2–23*

Mr. Hanson also tied for third prize in the 4th American Tourney (with the great Alfred Jordan, former Champion of England).

Index to Games

Grover won the choice and selected Whites for the first game. Thereafter the colors were reversed after every pair of games as is the custom under three-move restriction.

Grover   4 Wins   Hanson   2 Wins   Drawn   23

Winner and new Champion of the Pacific Coast

KENNETH M. GROVER

GAME 1

BLACK: J. B. Hanson		WHITE: Kenneth Grover	
9—13	19—16	6—10	6—2
24—19	12—19	21—17	25—29
11—15 A	23—16	13—22	16—12 G
28—24 B	15—18	26—17	29—25
6—9 C	26—22	10—15	31—27 G
22—18 D	1—6	18—14	23—26
15—22	22—15	15—18	20—16
25—18	10—19	14—9	11—20
9—14	25—22	18—22	2—11
18—9	4—8	17—13	25—22
5—14	22—18	22—25	27—24
29—25 E	14—23	9—6	20—27
8—11 F—Var. 1	27—18	2—9	32—23
24—20	8—11	13—6	Drawn
11—15	30—26	19—23	

Notes by KENNETH M. GROVER

A The opening moves are made and Jesse presses the button on his self-operating Time Clock. Jesse and I are dispensing with the five minute rule, long antique, and are utilizing a system whereby we each have twenty moves to make in one hour. We believe many moves require little thought, and others are

21

so difficult and delicate, needing much more than only five minutes to solve.

Our first opening is an old timer of the two move era where Black plays defensively. With all the knowledge at our disposal, the game often results in a rest period. This is a good opening to warm up to the improved system of keeping time. A player can now secure the benefit of accumulated time, making a move when he desires as long as he keeps within the time limit. At one time during the match I took a little over a half hour but the ensuing moves were made rapidly, both to make up for lost time and because I thought I hit upon the correct combination required for the position. Three move restriction especially needs more time in many cases because of so many lopsided openings.

The spectators enjoyed the spectacle of seeing us ponder over the difficult settings and then push the pieces quickly when the crisis was passed.

Our sister game "Chess" has long adhered to Time Clocks and with many leading checker players championing the cause I feel sure the tourneys and matches in the near future will accept this new trend.

B Keeping the formation solid—the favorite reply.

C Made to avoid a cramp. If 8—11, 23—18 is high voltage pressure and if the inferior 5—9 is made White replies 22—18 running into a strong White game arising from 9—13, 24—19, 5—9, 28—24, 11—15.

D The text and 23—18 are equal favorites. See game 2 for 23—18.

E Allowing Black choice. Most textbooks hew to 24—20 thus preventing 7—11. Often it is preferable to allow your opponent an array of lines to pick from making it more complicated for him. Often a forced line *forces* him to find the only means to

22

draw. The usual theme is for forced play but often allowing your opponent to go wrong with a little leeway is successful. In the above game either 29—25 or 24—20 is suitable.

F Black decides to stay on the regular path. See Variation 1 for 7—11.

G Getting ready for the clearance.

Variation 1

7—11	32—27 A	7—23	22—17
25—22	1—5 B	26—19	13—22
11—15	27—23	9—14	26—3
23—18	5—9	30—26	4—8
14—23	23—18	2—7	21—17
27—11	3—7	19—15 C	28—32
8—15	18—11	10—28	17—14

and 8—11, 3—8, 11—16, 8—11, 16—20, 11—15, 32—27. *Drawn*

A An awkward looking move varying from regular theory and published play. The late Sam Gonotsky offered: 26—23, 1—5, 32—28, 4—8, 23—18, 8—11, 31—26, 5—9, 21—17, 10—14, 17—10, 13—17, 22—6, 15—31, 6—1, 11—16, 19—15, 16—20, 24—19, 31—27, 1—5, 27—23, 10—6. *Drawn*

B 4—8, 27—23, 8—11, 23—18, 2—6, 21—17, 6—9, 17—14, 10—17, 19—10, 11—16, 24—19, 16—23, 26—19, 17—26, 31—22, 1—5, 18—15, 9—14, 10—7, 3—10, 15—6, 14—17, 22—18, 17—22, 18—14, 13—17. *White wins*

C 26—23, 14—17, 21—14, 10—26, 31—22, 7—10, 22—18, 4—8, 15—18, 12—16. *Drawn*

GAME 2

9—13, 24—19, 11—15

BLACK: Kenneth Grover WHITE: J. B. Hanson

9—13	32—28 A	6—10	13—6
24—19	11—16	23—18	2—9
11—15	19—15	10—15	21—17
28—24	10—19	22—17	11—16
6—9	24—15	13—22	17—13
23—18	3—7	26—17	9—14
1—6	30—26	15—22	18—9
18—11	7—11	25—18	5—14 D
7—23	15—8	16—19	
26—19	4—11 B	17—13	
8—11	27—23	19—23	Drawn

Notes by KENNETH M. GROVER

A The general theme that starts now and ends at B should be carefully noted. Similar positions often arise and the ideas can be used from this game. In using theory always try to look through the position and do not be satisfied unless you can find a reason for your move. Too often a sound looking formation boomerangs from not being wary for some odd looking move.

B A case of similar position with this theme from A is 9—14, 24—20, 5—9, 22—18, 10—15, 28—24, 15—22, 26—10, 7—14, 25—22, 1—5 C, 22—17, 14—18, 23—14, 9—18, 30—26, 3—7, 26—22, 18—25, 29—22 C.

24

C Notice the similarity (with colors reversed).

D A hurdy-gurdy game played a multitude of times under two move. Originally contested between Jordan and Barker and is the trunk game in Kear's Encyclopedia.

GAME 3

11—16, 22—18, 7—11

BLACK: Kenneth Grover WHITE: J. B. Hanson

11—16	17—21	2—7 L	13—17
22—18	31—27	25—22	7—10
7—11 A	5—9 J	7—10	17—22
25—22 B—Var. 1	27—24	26—23	11—7
3—7	7—10 K	11—15	22—25
29—25	15—6	19—16	7—2
16—19	1—10	15—19	25—29
24—15	18—15 K	22—18	2—7
10—19	10—19	19—26	29—25
23—16	24—15	18—9	7—11
12—19	11—18	26—31	25—22
21—17 C	22—15	9—6	11—16
9—13 D	8—11 K	10—15	22—17
17—14 E	15—8	6—2	16—20
6—10 F	4—11	15—19	31—27
27—24 G	28—24	16—11	10—15
10—17	9—14	19—23	17—13 M
24—15	24—19	2—7	Drawn

Notes by KENNETH M. GROVER

A Up to the present White has done well with the power given him in this exciting three mover. With most of the choice White tracks down a favorable mid-game.

We predict that in the immediate future, the constant pounding by the experts and analysts will lead Black to the correct procedure of softening White's offensive thrusts.

B White has three good routes. The text and 18–14 are choice morsels while 24–19 has a share of winning possibilities. 11–16, 22–18, 7–11 should be your master game in the studying of the following four openings.

(1) 11–16, 22–18, 7–11
(2) 11–16, 22–17, 7–11
(3) 11–16, 24–19, 7–11
(4) 10–15, 22–17, 7–10

11–16, 22–18, 7–11, 18–14 is the same as 11–16, 22–17, 7–11, 17–14. 11–16, 22–18, 7–11, 24–19 reproduces into 11–16, 24–19, 7–11, 22–18, 10–15, 22–17, 7–10, 17–14, 10–17, 21–14, 9–18, 23–14, 11–16 can easily transpose into the following: 11–16, 22–18, 7–11, 18–14, 10–17, 21–14, 9–18, 23–14, 11–15; and 11–16, 22–17, 7–11, 18–14, 10–17, 21–14, 9–18, 23–14, 11–15.

C For 18–15 see game 4.

D Rated as the star move.

E White may juggle the position by moving 25–21. Move 6–10, 17–14, 10–17, 21–14, 1–6, 27–24, 11–15, 18–11, 8–15, and we have Note *G* at the 8th move.

F An important key move.

G Harold Freyer and I had the following continuation at the 10th American Championship tourney: 25–21, 10–17, 21–14, 1–6, 27–24, 11–15, 18–11, 8–15, 14–10, 7–14, 22–18, 14–23, 31–27, 15–18, 24–15, 4–8, 26–19, 2–7, 28–24, 8–12, 27–23 *H*, 18–27, 32–23, 13–17, 24–20, 17–22, 15–11, 7–16, 20–11, 22–26. *Drawn*

H Up to this point the play is by George W. Bass. Freyer

27

sensed that I had been over this play and made a stab that gave me easy sailing. Preferable would be 24–20, 18–22, 27–23 (Ryan's continuation), 22–26, 15–11, 7–16, 20–11, 26–31, 23–18, 6–10, 11–7, 5–9 (Bradford's 5–9 move and improves Ryan's 10–14 draw), 7–2, 10–14, 18–15, 14–18, 2–6, 9–14, 6–9, 18–23, 9–27, 31–24, 30–25, 13–17, 25–21, 17–22, 21–17, 22–26, 17–14, 26–31, 14–10, 31–26, 10–7, 26–22, 7–2, 22–18. *Drawn*

J Varies from published play and is satisfactory. We append a diagram after the 5–9 move.

BOTH NEED RELEASE

WHITE (Hanson) 32, 30, 28, 27, 26, 25, 22, 18, 15

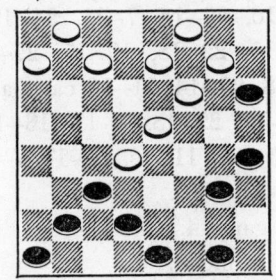

BLACK (Grover) 1, 2, 4, 7, 8, 9, 11, 13, 21

White to Play

In lieu of 5–9, 7–10 is the move taken in a game between W. T. Dailey and W. C. Crook. It continued 15–6, 1–10, 27–24, 11–15, 18–11, 8–15, 24–19, 15–24, 28–19, 10–14, 19–16, 2–7, 22–18, 14–23, 26–19, 13–17, 19–15, 4–8, 32–27, 5–9, 27–24, 9–14, 24–19, 14–18, 16–12, 8–11, 15–8, 7–11, 8–3, 11–16, 19–15, 17–22. *Drawn*

K Although White is best, both sides have to release a cramp.

L Hanson's position looks stronger than it actually is. Although I tread a narrow groove one good move is all I ask for.

M The spectators had me down for the count but White cannot attack this bridge.

Variation 1

17–14 *A*	17–14 *C D*	21–14	18–11
10–17	8–11	12–16	26–31
21–14	15–8	26–23	11–7
9–18	4–11	16–19	9–14
23–14	28–24	23–16	7–2
11–15 *B–Var. 2*	11–15	7–10	31–26
25–22	30–26	14–7	2–6
16–19	3–7	2–20	14–18
22–18	29–25	31–26	6–10
15–22	1–6	5–9	26–23
24–15	32–28	26–23	10–14
6–9	6–10	18–22 *F*	23–32
26–17	25–21	23–18	14–23
9–18	10–17	22–26	20–27
			Drawn

A An aggressive line placing a strong man on square 14. This play also arises from 11–16, 22–17, 17–14 and was the method of the start of the game with Long in the semi-finals of the 10th American Checker Association tourney for the United States Championship at Flint, Michigan. See game number 20 for additional play.

B I favor this defense but 3–7 as given in Variation 2 has merit also.

C At the 10th A.C.A. tourney I essayed 28–24 against Harold Freyer, the hard fighting New Yorker, now stationed overseas. After 28–24 our game continued: 5–9, 17–14, 9–13, 29–25, 12–16, 31–26, 16–19, 32–28, 13–17, 25–22, 18–25, 30–21, 3–7, 15–10, 7–11, 24–15, 11–18, 10–6, 2–9, 14–5, 18–22, 21–14, 22–31, 14–10, 31–24, 28–19, 8–11. *Drawn*

D Playing Black against the late H. B. Reynolds at the same tourney, he ventured 29–25. We drew as follows: 29–25, 8–11, 15–8, 4–11, 28–24, 11–15, 17–14, 3–7, 30–26, 1–6, (now same as Variation 1 at 24th move), 26–23, 6–10, 23–19 *E*, 10–17, 19–3, 17–21, 3–8, 21–30, 27–23, 18–27, 32–23, 30–25, 8–11, 25–22, 11–15, 5–9, 15–19, 22–25, 23–18, 9–13, 18–14, 25–22, 14–9, 22–18, 9–5, 13–17, 5–1, 18–14, 1–5, 17–21, 24–20, 21–25, 19–15, 25–29.

E 25–21, 10–17, 21–14, 18–22, 23–18, 22–25, 18–11, 7–11. *Drawn*

F 9–14, 23–19, 14–17, 19–10, 17–22, 10–7, 22–26, 7–2, 26–31, 2–7, 31–26, 7–10, 26–23, draws on the same theme as the trunk.

Variation 2

BLACK: Asa Long		WHITE: Kenneth Grover	
3–7 *A*	26–23	1–6	17–13
25–21	19–26	27–23	11–15
11–15	30–14	18–27	28–24
29–25	15–19 *B–Var. 3*	32–23	15–18
16–19	24–15	8–11	24–20
25–22	7–10	21–17	18–27
6–9	14–7	6–9 *D*	31–24
22–17	2–18	14–10	14–18
9–18	17–14 *C*	9–14 *E*	10–7

18–23	31–27	32–27	32–28
7–2	6–2	19–24	23–19
23–27	16–20	27–32	28–32
2–7	7–11	24–28	19–15
27–32	27–23	31–27	32–27
24–19	2–7	11–15	15–10
32–28	23–27	27–31	27–24
19–15	12–8	15–18	10–14
28–24	27–24	4–8	9–13
7–10	8–3	18–23	18–22
24–28	24–28	31–27	24–27
10–14	7–2	14–18	14–18
28–24	28–32	8–11	27–32
14–10*R*	3–8	28–24	18–23
24–28	32–28	11–15	32–28
15–11	8–12	24–31	23–27
12–16	28–32	15–22	28–32
11–7	11–7	23–26*S*	22–26
16–19	20–24	22–25	32–23
7–3	12–16	26–30	26–19
19–23	32–27	25–29	13–17
3–7	7–11	20–24	19–23
23–26	27–23	32–27	17–21
20–16	16–20	24–19	23–18
26–31	23–27	27–32	29–25
10–14	2–7	19–23	30–26
28–24	24–28	32–28	25–29
16–12	11–16	31–27	18–22*T*
24–20	28–32	5–9	
13–9	7–11	23–18	
20–16	27–31	28–32	*Black*
9–6	16–19	27–23	*Resigned*

31

A Much publicity has been given my win over Long enabling me to snare a heat and almost win the American Championship. This is the first time the game has been published. The position now is the same as the 3–8 line of the Paisley Bust usually arriving from 11–16, 22–18, 8–11, 18–14, 10–17, 21–14, 9–18, 23–14, 3–8. Although the line was sometimes taken in the two move era, the modern performers are developing their own model structures.

B With this move Black begins his downfall. I can find no draw after 15–19 is made. See Variation 3 and also ninth move of Ryan's Note *C* of the 20th game.

C 27–23 has been published to draw. 17–14 cramps down hard on Black's weakened position. Black has his pieces scattered. White holds some of these pieces on the side to secure the winning ending.

D In the 3rd N.C.A. mail tourney Bixby and Easton played 11–15, 23–19 to draw. In lieu of 23–19, move 14–10, 6–9, 17–13, 9–14, 28–24 and we transpose into the Long-Grover game five moves hence.

E The position is starting to fume so let's place a diagram on this page.

KEEPING CONTROL

BLACK (Long) 4, 5, 9, 11, 12

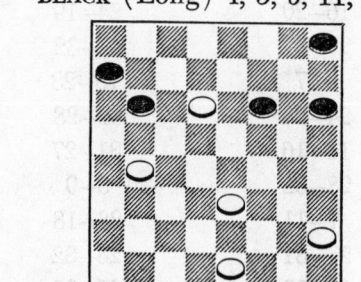

WHITE (Grover) 31, 28, 23, 17, 10

Black to Play

Long may have given a harder tussle by 9–13, 17–14, 11–15F, 10–7, 15–18, 7–2, 18–27, 31–24, 4–8N, 24–20, 13–17, 2–6, 8–11O, 14–10, 11–15, 10–7, 15–18, 6–10, 18–22, 10–14, 17–21, 14–17, 22–25, 17–22, 25–30, 22–26, 29–25, 6–2, 5–9, 28–24, 9–13P, 26–30, 25–22, 2–6, 22–18, 6–9, 18–15, 9–14, 13–17, 30–26. *White wins*

After Black makes his move on the diagrammed position a study in timing is in the offing. White holds enough to win but can muff his opportunity if he does not co-ordinate his pieces toward the correct attack.

F 13–17, 10–7, 17–22G, 7–3, 11–16, 3–7, 4–8, 7–10, 18–22, 10–15, 16–20, 23–19, 25–30, 14–10, 5–9, 10–7, 9–14, 7–3, 14–17, 3–7, 17–22, 28–24, 20–27, 31–24, 30–26, 7–11, 26–23, 11–4, 23–16, 24–20. *White wins*

G The position had me engrossed and I was getting a bit woozy so I asked Hanson, whom I meet every evening at 11 P.M. at the Todd Shipyard before we start our day, to look at the possibilities of 11–15. The next evening he brought in the following to vanquish any hopes for it. 11–15, (Position can run into Note E at 5th move if Black elects to move 13–17 instead of 15–18 in that setting.) 7–2Q, 15–18H, I, 2–7, 18–27, 31–24, 12–16, 7–11, 16–20, 24–19, 20–24, 19–15, 24–27, 15–10, 27–31, 10–6, 31–26, 6–2, 26–22, 2–6, 22–18K, 6–9, 18–22, 9–13, 17–21, 28–24, 21–25, 24–20, 25–30, 20–16, 30–26, 16–12, 26–23, 12–8. *White wins*

H 15–19, 23–16, 12–19, 2–6, 4–8, 6–10, 8–11, 10–7, 11–16, 7–11, 16–20, 31–26. *White wins*–Hanson

J 12–16, 2–7, 17–22, 14–9, 5–14, 7–10. *White wins*–Hanson

K 17–21, 14–10, 22–17, 10–7, 17–13, 7–2, 21–25, 28–24, 25–30, 24–20, 30–25, 20–16, 25–22, 16–12, 22–18, 12–8,

18–22, 8–3, 22–18, 3–8, 18–22, 8–12, 22–18, 12–16, 18–22 L, 16–19, 22–18, 2–7, 18–22, (if 13–17, 19–15, 18–22, 7–10, *White wins*), 19–15, 22–17, 15–18, 17–21, 18–14, 13–17, 7–10, 17–13, 11–15, 13–17, 15–18, 4–8, 6–9. *White wins*

L 5–9, 16–19, 18–22 M, 19–23, 22–17, 23–18, 17–21, 18–22, 21–17, 6–1, 17–26, 1–5, 26–23, 5–14, 23–19, 14–9. *White wins by first position.*

M 9–14, 19–23, 18–27, 6–9 *and White again wins by first position.*

N 12–16, 2–7, 16–20, 24–19, 20–24, 7–11, 24–27, 11–15, 27–32, 15–18, 4–8, 19–15, 32–27 (if 8–12, 18–23, *White wins*), 15–10, 8–11, 10–7, 11–16, 7–2, 16–19, 2–6, 27–32, 28–24, 19–28, 18–23, 13–17, 6–10. *White wins*

O 17–22, 14–10, 22–26, 10–7, 26–30, 6–10, 30–26, 10–15, 26–22, 6–2, 5–9, 2–7, 9–14, 7–11, 22–18, 15–22, 8–15, 28–24, 14–18, 22–26. *White wins*

P 9–14 loses by 2–6, 14–17, 26–30, 25–22, 6–9. *White wins*

Q A likely looking sequence to beware of is 28–24, 15–18, 24–20, 18–27, 31–24, 17–22, 7–2, 4–8, 24–19, 22–26, 19–15, 26–30, 2–7, 30–26, 7–11, 26–22, 11–4, 22–18. *Drawn.* This draw might arise by a different order of moves on other attacks.

R Black is in a vise. Repeating the moves with an object of gaing more time, although my plan was to allow Black to move 12–16 shortly. I had this position in mind for many a move.

S The wary Long forces me to win it this way as any other move allows a draw. Try 23–18, 22–25, 31–26, 25–30, 26–22, 5–9, 22–17, 9–13, 17–22, 32–28, 18–23, 28–32, 20–24, 32–28, 23–19, 28–32, 24–28, 32–27. *Drawn.* A case where having the move is a liability.

T The longest game of the tourney even gave the official timekeeper, and scorer, Mervin Wride, a test of patience. Another recommendation for the Time Clock system.

Variation 3

BLACK: Freyer   WHITE: Loew

7–11	26–22	18–14	10–7
14–9	27–31	9–5	18–22
5–14	23–19	14–18	27–23
17–10	15–24	7–3	22–26
11–16 A	28–19	18–22	7–10
21–17	31–27	3–7	26–22
16–19	10–7	22–18	10–7
31–26	26–30	32–27	22–26
12–16	22–18	18–22	7–3
27–23	30–26	7–10	26–22
8–12	17–13	22–18	3–7
24–20	26–22	10–7	22–26 C
19–24	18–14	18–22 B	
20–11	22–18	7–10	
24–27	14–9	22–18	Draw

A Varies from 13th move of Note C of game 20 where 15–19 is given. The above game appears sound but the preference is 15–19, a tested reply.

B Repeating moves to gain time is like a prize fighter waiting for the count of nine.

C A see-saw draw.

35

GAME 4

11–16, 22–18, 7–11

BLACK: J. B. Hanson   WHITE: Kenneth Grover

11–16	27–23*C*–*Var. 1*	2–6	15–10
22–18	8–12	25–21	1–5
7–11	23–16	9–14	10–6
25–22	12–19	27–24	14–18
3–7	32–27	18–23	6–2
29–25	4–8	13–9	18–23
16–19	27–23	6–13	28–24
24–15	8–12	15–10	23–26
10–19	23–16	23–27	30–23
23–16	12–19	24–15	13–17
12–19	31–27	27–31	21–14
18–15*A*	14–18*D*	10–3	9–27
11–18	21–17	31–22	24–19
22–15	6–9*E*	3–7	
9–14*B*	17–13*K*	5–9	Drawn

Notes by KENNETH M. GROVER

A Varies from the preceding game and has considerable potency.

B The main defense: 7–11 is strongly attacked by 27–24.

C A subtle attack that has more power than first impressions would suppose. A model game is Variation 1.

36

D Black can work out a draw with the following:

5—9	3—8	23—30	18—9
27—23	27—31	16—23	25—29
7—10	25—22	1—5	9—5
23—16	9—14	28—24	22—25
10—19	8—11	5—9	5—1
16—11	31—27	24—19	25—30
14—18	11—16	9—13	1—5
11—8	27—23	25—22	30—25
18—23	22—17	30—25	23—26
8—3	6—10	22—18	10—14
23—27	30—25	13—22	*Drawn*

E Black makes the star move. We append a diagram before the ungainly 6—9 is made.

A STUDY IN BLACK AND WHITE

BLACK (Hanson) 1, 2, 5, 6, 7, 18, 19

WHITE (Grover) 15, 17, 25, 26, 27, 28, 30

Black to Play

7—10 loses by 17—13, 10—14*F*, 15—11, 5—9*G*, 27—24, 18—23, 24—15, 23—27, 26—22, 14—17 (if 26—30, 25—21, 14—18, 21—17, *White wins*), 22—18, 17—22, 25—21, 27—32, 11—7, 2—11, 15—8,

37

32–27, 21–17, 27–23, 17–14, 1–5, 28–24, 23–27 (if 22–26, 24–19, *White wins*), 8–3, 27–20, 3–7, 20–24 *H*, 14–10, 6–15, 18–11, 9–14, 7–10, 14–17, 10–14, 17–21, 14–18. *White wins*

F Moving 5–9 and allowing White a three for two shot is a futile effort. 5–9, 26–23, 19–26, 30–5, 10–19, 25–22, 6–10, 22–17, 10–15, 27–24, 19–23, 24–19, 15–24, 28–19, 23–26, 17–14, 26–30, 14–10, 30–26, 19–16, 26–23, 16–11, 23–18, 10–7, 18–14, 7–3, 14–10, 11–8, 10–6, 8–4, 6–10, 4–8, 10–6, 8–11, 6–10, 3–8, 10–6, 8–12, 6–10, 12–16, 10–6, 16–19, 6–10, 11–15, 10–7, 19–16, 2–6, 16–19, 7–2 *J*, 15–11, 6–10, 13–9, 10–14 (if 1–6, 11–7, *White wins*), 19–23, 1–6, 11–7, 6–13, 7–10, 14–17, 23–18. *White wins*

G If 6–10, 11–8, 10–15, 8–3, 5–9, 13–6, 1–10, 26–23, 19–26, 30–23, and White can win easily.

H 6–10 also goes down for the count by 13–6, 10–17, 7–10, 20–24, 10–14, 17–21, 14–17, 22–25, 17–22, 25–29, 18–14, 24–19, 6–1 and White can win by holding two pieces on the side and the King on 29, with two Kings.

J If 7–10, 13–9, 6–13, 15–6, 1–10, 5–1, 10–14, 19–15, 14–17, 15–18, 17–21, 18–22. *White wins*

K 17–14 could surely be dynamite the first time met in match play. Black can easily go astray. The correct play would be 2–6 *L*, only drawable move, 27–24, 19–23 (the only key to the combination), 26–19, 6–10, 15–6, 1–17, 19–15, 17–21, 24–20, 9–13, 20–16, 13–17, 28–24, 5–9 *M*, 24–20, 9–13, 16–12, 17–22, 12–8, 22–29, 8–3, 7–11, 15–8, 13–17, 3–7, 17–22, 7–10, 18–23. Draw analyzed by Jesse B. Hanson after I suggested 17–14 as a powerhouse.

L The natural 1–6 loses by the following fireworks: 27–24, 9–13 (18–23, 16–11, *White wins*). 15–11, 7–16, 24–15, 16–19, 14–10, 6–9, 10–7, 2–11, 15–8, 18–23, 8–3, 23–27, 3–7, 27–31, 25–22, 9–14 (if 31–27, 7–10, 27–24, 19–26,

38

28–19 *and White can win*), 7–10, 5–9, 10–17, 31–27, 17–21, 9–14, 21–25, 27–31N, 26–23, 19–26, 30–23, 14–17, 25–30, 17–26, 23–18.

M Black is now safe enough and can easily draw by the alternate 18–23, 24–20, 23–27, 25–22.

N 27–32 also loses by 25–29O, 32–27, 26–23, 27–25, 29–22, White holding two pieces with the King to win.

O Beware of 26–23, 19–26, 30–23, 14–17, 22–18, 17–22, 25–21, 32–27. *Drawn*

Variation 1

L. M. Lewis *vs.* N. Rubin

25–22 A	25–29	24–15	2–11
14–18	27–24	18–22	14–10
22–17	7–11	17–14	22–25
18–22	15–10	11–18	30–21
17–14	6–15	26–17	29–25
22–25	14–10	18–22	*Drawn*
21–17	15–18	10–7	

A Rubin and Lewis had this interesting by-play. 15–11, 7–16, 27–24, 5–9, 24–15, 16–19, 32–27, 2–7, 27–23, 8–12, 23–16, 12–19, 25–22, 7–11, 15–8, 4–11, 31–27, 9–13, 27–24, 11–15, 26–23, 19–26, 30–23, 15–19, 23–16, 6–9, 16–11, 1–5. *Drawn*

39

GAME 5

10—15, 23—18, 7—10

BLACK: J. B. Hanson		WHITE: Kenneth Grover	
10—15	11—18	18—25	18—23
23—18	22—15	29—22	17—14
7—10 A	7—11	6—10	10—17
27—23 B	27—24	22—17	21—14
3—7	11—18	5—9	11—16
32—27 C	24—15	17—13	24—20
15—19	9—14	10—15	16—19
24—15	28—24	13—6	20—16
10—19	8—11	1—10	23—27
23—16	15—8	26—22	31—24
12—19	4—11	14—18	19—28
18—15 D	25—22 H	22—17	Drawn

Notes by KENNETH M. GROVER

A White has an inconsiderable amount of leeway in choice of lines.

B 26—23, 10—14, 23—19 leads to simplicity. This text is also devoid of complications on many avenues.

C It can be noted that this opening often arose during the early "go as you please era" sometimes arising by the above order of moves and more often from 11—15, 23—18, 7—11, 27—23, 3—7, 32—27 to the above position. A game that has stood the test of time between Dearborn and Ferrie ran as

40

follows: Instead of 32–27 move 24–20, 15–19, 23–16, 12–19, 18–15, 11–18, 22–15, 9–14, 25–22, 7–11, 29–25, 11–18, 22–15, 5–9, 32–27, 9–13, 27–23, 8–12, 23–16, 10–19, 25–22, 6–10, 16–11, 12–16, 28–24. *Drawn*

D 22–17, 9–13, 17–14, 6–9E, 27–24, 11–15, 18–11, 8–15, 21–17, 9–18, 26–23, 18–27, 24–20, 13–22, 25–11, 7–16, 31–15, 16–19. *Drawn by Shearer*

E Weaker is 11–15, 18–11, 8–15, 21–17, 13–22, 25–11, 7–16, 27–24, 6–9, 24–15, 9–18, 15–11, 1–6, 29–25, 6–10, 31–27, and is a problem position given in the original British Draught Player with Black to play and draw. A recent textbook also dramatizes this end game which arises from a modern three move opening. Those old timers can still teach us. Continue 5–9F, 26–23, 9–14G, 28–24, 10–15, 24–20, 15–19, 25–21, 19–26, 30–23, 18–22, 27–24, 22–26, 24–19, 14–18, 23–14, 16–23, 14–10, 26–30, 21–**17**, 30–26, 17–13, 26–22, 10–6. *Drawn*

F 10–15 draws by 26–23, 18–22, 25–18, 15–22, 23–18, 16–19, 18–14, 2–6, 11–7, 6–9, 14–10, 9–14, 7–3, 14–18. *Gardner*

G B.D.P. offers a White win if 10–14 is made. Continue 30–26, 9–13, 26–22, 14–17, 22–15, 17–21, 25–22, 21–25, 22–18, 25–30, 11–8.

H Paves the way for the draw and not as aggressive as 24–19 as played by Hanson in the next game.

GAME 6

10—15, 23—18, 7—10

BLACK: Kenneth Grover   WHITE: J. B. Hanson

10—15	28—24	5—14	29—25
23—18	8—11	17—10	26—23
7—10	15—8	27—23	25—21
27—23	4—11	25—22	23—26
3—7	24—19 A	15—19	14—9
32—27	11—15	21—17	26—22
15—19	19—10	19—24	9—6 N
24—15	6—15	17—13	22—15
10—19	26—22 B	24—27	21—17
23—16	18—23 D	30—25	2—9
12—19	22—17 F	27—31	13—6
18—15	14—18	25—21	15—18
11—18	31—26 J	23—19	6—2
22—15	23—27	22—18	18—14
7—11	26—23	31—26	17—13
27—24	27—31	21—17	14—7
11—18	23—14	26—23 K	2—11
24—15	31—27	17—14	1—5
9—14	14—9	23—26	*Black Wins*

Notes by KENNETH M. GROVER

A Places Black on the defensive.

B The following setting, before 26—22 is made, oozes with possibilities for exciting play.

SO SUBTLE

BLACK (Grover) 1, 2, 5, 14, 15, 18

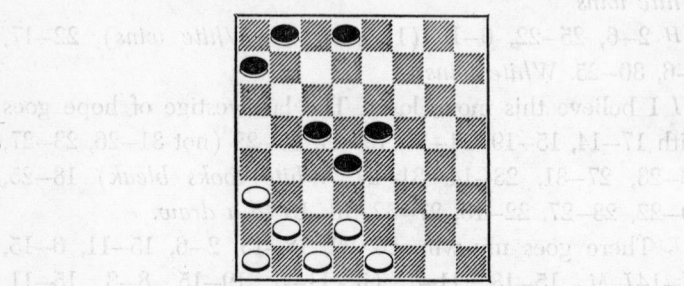

WHITE (Hanson) 21, 25, 26, 29, 30, 31

White to Play

Tricky is 25—22, 18—25, 29—22, 15—19, 31—27, 1—6 *C*, 22—17, 6—10, 26—22, 5—9, 27—23, 19—26, 30—23, 9—13, 23—19, 14—18, 22—6, 2—9, 19—15. *Drawn*

C A lost cause is 5—9, 22—17, 2—6, 17—10, 6—15, 21—17, 9—13, 17—14, 15—18, 14—10, 18—22, 26—17, 13—22, 10—7, 1—5, 7—2, 5—9, 2—7, 9—14, 7—10, 14—18, 10—14, 19—23, 27—24, 22—26, 24—20. *White wins*

D Looking for some freedom of the pieces. A bad move is 1—6, followed by 31—27, 5—9, 30—26, 9—13 *E*, 27—24, 6—9, 24—20, 2—6, 20—16, 6—10, 16—11, 18—23, 26—19, 15—24, 11—7, 24—27, 7—2. *White wins*

E 6—10, 27—24, 2—6, 22—17, 9—13, 26—23. *White wins*

F Hanson is overreaching the value of his game. A surprise to me was his aggressiveness as Jesse was known as a safe book player. His last hope of winning is based on 22—18,

15–22, 25–9, 5–14, 29–25, 2–7 *G,H*, 25–22, 7–11, 22–17, 14–18, 17–14, 11–16, 14–10, 16–20, 10–7, 23–27, 31–24, 20–27, 7–3, 27–32, 21–17, 32–27, 17–14. *Drawn.* The tide has turned with the 22–17 move.

G 1–6, 25–22, 6–9 (2–7, 22–17, 14–18 *Draws*), 30–25, *White wins*

H 2–6, 25–22, 6–10 (1–5, 30–25, *White wins*), 22–17, 1–6, 30–25. *White wins*

J I believe this move loses. The last vestige of hope goes with 17–14, 15–19, 14–10, 19–24, 25–22 (not 31–26, 23–27, 26–23, 27–31, 23–14, 31–27, *White looks bleak*) 18–25, 29–22, 23–27, 22–18, 27–32, 18–15 *to a draw.*

K There goes my win. 26–22, 18–15, 2–6, 15–11, 6–15, 17–14 *L,M*, 15–18, 11–7 (if 11–8, 19–15, 8–3, 15–11, *Black wins*), 22–25, 29–15, 19–3, 13–9, 3–7, 9–5, 1–6, 5–1, 6–9, 14–5, 7–10! *Black wins*

L 11–8, 19–16, 8–3, 16–11. *Black wins*

M 11–7, 22–25, 29–22, 15–18, 22–15, 19–3, 17–14, 3–7, 13–9, 7–2, 9–5, 2–6. *Black wins*

N Into the soup. 18–15, 22–18, 9–6 draws, and nothing can be done about it. I noted that 26–23 would force 18–15 for the same draw so clung to the last straw and moved 26–22.

GAME 7

10–15, 23–19, 7–10

BLACK: Kenneth Grover   WHITE: J. B. Hanson

10–15	22–17 H	22–25	2–7
23–19	8–11	14–10	19–24
7–10 A	19–16 H	25–29	7–11
22–18 B	12–19	2–6 K	24–27
15–22	23–7	29–25	11–15
25–18	2–11	6–9	27–31
11–15 C	26–23 H	25–22	10–7
18–11	3–8	9–14	31–26
8–15	31–27	22–17	15–19
21–17 D	8–12	13–9	22–25
9–14 E	23–18 J	15–19 L	19–24
17–13	14–23	9–6	26–31
14–17 E	27–18	11–15	13–17
29–25	10–15	6–2	1–6 M
17–21 E	18–14	19–23	7–3
25–22 F	15–18	2–6	6–10
5–9	14–9	17–13	3–7
27–23 F	6–10	6–2	10–15
9–14	9–6	13–17	7–11
24–20 F	10–15	14–9	
15–24	6–2	15–19	*White Wins*
28–19	18–22	9–13	
4–8 G	17–14	17–22	

45

Notes by TOMMIE WISWELL

A An old friend, frequently played under two move restriction and go-as-you-please. Despite its familiarity it is still producing wins, as this game well illustrates. Mr. Hanson is recognized as the world's outstanding authority on these old games, in fact, we would say that he is easily entitled to be called "The unrestricted Champion of the World." . . . He is one of the few remaining Masters of another era which included such immortals as Matty Priest, Alfred Jordan, Hugh Henderson, Doctor August Schaeffer, Johnnie Horr, and Gus Heffner.

Jesse and Newell Banks are the two outstanding Masters who serve as connecting links between the players of yesteryear and today. Both deserve much praise for their continued activity and ability to keep in step with Twentieth Century Checkers.

B This would also be our choice here as 22—17 would run into an old line (which usually came up in former days via 11—15, 23—19, 7—11, 22—17 same) and is scarcely a game White could hope to score with. Incidentally, on this line, after 22—17, a favorite of ours is the "Dodger line" which avoids the run-of-the-mill variation. After 22—17 play 11—16, 26—23, 8—11! and now White must play 17—14 and we have a wide open game. It was also a favorite of the late Samuel Gonotsky, former Champion of America and one of the greatest players of all time.

C While not the fatal move for Black this is inferior to 9—14 as played in the next game. We would label it an unwise choice for use in important match play.

D Let's take a look at this maneuver as it has a lot of subtle strength which the student probably does not grasp at once.

Note that with this move, and his next one, White makes two good developing moves *without "disturbing" or weakening his position,* yet, though his formation is "intact," it is not cramped or clogged up—as Black's definitely is in a few moves.

It might also be mentioned here that, as a rule, it is poor checkers for Black to occupy squares 21 and 28 (the same holds true for White with regards to squares 5 and 12, the dog-holes). However, a man on 13 or 20 is often to be desired as there it serves as a slight cramp on the opposing double corner. The weakness of men on 21 and 28 (and 12 and 5) lies in the fact that they are often literally "out of the game" and are sometimes referred to as "dead men." We like to call them "Zombies" for though they remain on the board their effect is frequently nil. Many famous "man down" draws are the result of pieces winding up on these ill-fated squares.

Like all theories in Checkers there are exceptions to this rule which only constant practice and study will enable the student to recognize.

E These moves form the fatal weak link in the Black game. 4–8, 17–13, 8–11, 29–25, etc. will draw but by playing 9–14 at note C, as in the next game, Black avoids unnecessary trouble.

F From now on the weakness of Black's man on 21 and the strength of White's piece on 13 become apparent, even to the fledgling tenderfoot. However, it is a bit too late for Black to do much about it. All his squirming and wiggling avails him naught. There is something awesome about the finality and absolute precision of master Checkers which is extremely fascinating. In Chess, slight errors in judgment are often overcome, even against master players. This is due to the wider range of play and greater freedom of movement. But in Checkers, one of the few exact sciences known to man, the

slightest departure from precise play (amongst experts) results in the loss of an otherwise perfectly played game.

It is the perfect game because it calls for perfection and none of us are perfect. It is at one and the same time entertaining and enlightening.

G In my exhibition games I am always amazed at the number of players who insist upon playing 3–7 in formations of this type, entirely overlooking the simple shot by 13–9, 6–13, 19–15, 10–19, 23–16, 12–19, 22–17, 13–22, 26–3. *White wins*

H The weakness and treachery of the man on 21 becomes more and more apparent as the game proceeds. It is not only of little value to Black but actually is of infinite assistance to White as a "pillar" or "leaning post." Contrast the freedom and mobility of the White forces with the restricted character of Black's position, due primarily to the "black sheep" on 21.

J Star move to win. 27–24 and 23–19 only draw. 27–24 (23–19, 11–15, 27–24 same) 11–15, 23–19, 15–18, 20–16 (32–28, 18–23, 19–15, 10–19, 24–15, 23–27, 17–10, 27–31 draws), 18–23, 16–11, 23–26!, 30–23, 21–25, 11–7, 14–21, 7–3, 25–30 (or 10–14) 3–7, 10–15, 19–10, 6–15, 7–10, 30–26, 10–19, 12–16. *Drawn*

K White figured that if he crowned the man on 10 now he would still have difficulty in attacking the men on 11 and 15.

L 17–13, 10–7, 13–6, 7–2 a neat "pincers" movement that would have brought matters to a hasty conclusion.

M A forlorn hope for 7–2, 23–26, 30–23 (2–9, 25–22), 31–26, 2–9, 26–28. *Drawn*

GAME 8

10–15, 23–19, 7–10

BLACK: J. B. Hanson   WHITE: Kenneth Grover

10–15	24–20	8–12	21–14
23–19	15–24	26–23	1–17 D
7–10	28–19	11–15	31–26 D
22–18 Var. 1	8–11 B	22–17	7–10
15–22	19–16	9–6 C	20–16
25–18	12–19	17–13	12–19
9–14 A	23–7	3–7 C	26–22
18–9	2–11	13–6	17–26
5–14	29–25	14–18	30–16 E
27–23 B	4–8	23–14	
11–15	25–22	10–17	Drawn

Notes by TOMMIE WISWELL

A Black sets the tempo of the game with this move, which makes it even sailing from here out. Black has several other choices here. 11–16, 10–15 and 9–13 are all drawable.

B The game now runs along a very familiar pattern, well known to both players.

C Working into a snap draw that arises in numerous games and will often save a game that appears hopeless. It is not necessary for the student to memorize such games as this, move for move. What is important is that he retain such ideas

49

and themes and learn to recognize them as they arise in actual play, as in this game. They occur in similar patterns out of a variety of openings and if the student grasps this lesson early in his career he will make rapid advancement as a player.

D Though White's King row now looks strong (against Black's scattered forces), the fact of the matter is that he can't stand still—he must make moves—and therein lies Black's salvation. A bridge position is strong only if there are other pieces on the board with which to force a winning continuation. Here it is only a pretty picture—momentarily.

E Probably not an exciting game for the seasoned expert, but one from which the student can learn much that is of real value. The study of basic formations such as this, which may occur in many games, from a variety of openings, will provide the necessary foundation upon which to build a consistently strong game.

Variation 1

22–17 A	27–2	17–14	7–11
9–14 A	20–27	4–8	16–20
25–22	32–16	29–25	11–16
11–16	6–9	8–11	19–23
26–23	16–12	25–22	16–19
16–20	8–11	6–10	23–26
30–26	2–6	14–7	19–23
2–7	11–15	3–10	26–30
23–18	6–13	12–8	22–17
14–30	1–6	10–15	*Drawn*
19–16	28–24	8–3	
12–19	15–18	11–16	
31–26	22–15	3–7	
30–23	10–28	15–19	

A Forming the "Whilter," one of the best known of the "go-as-you-please" games. The name obviously refers to the many exchanges and general tumult and confusion which marks many of its variations. Because of the widespread familiarity of the above game and the resultant scarcity of wins the line is often avoided by match and tourney players. It should, however, be thoroughly studied and understood by the student. 26—23 is sometimes played and is shown in variation 2.

Variation 2

C. F. Barker *vs.* J. P. Reed

26—23	24—20	27—23	11—7
9—14	15—24	6—9	15—19
22—18	28—19	22—17	7—2
15—22	11—15	9—13	10—15
25—9	32—28	23—19	17—14
5—14	15—24	13—22	22—25
29—25	28—19	26—17	21—17
11—15	8—11	14—18	25—29
25—22	19—16	19—16	2—7
8—11	12—19	11—15	*Drawn*
30—26	23—7	16—11	
4—8	2—11	18—22	

GAME 9

9—13, 23—19, 11—16

BLACK: J. B. Hanson   WHITE: Kenneth Grover

9—13	7—11 D	10—15	18—23
23—19	29—25	13—9	17—14
11—16 A	11—15	19—24	11—16
27—23 Var. 1	19—16	32—28	21—17
10—14 B	12—19	7—10	23—27
22—17 C	23—16	28—19	31—24
13—22	2—7	15—24	16—20
25—9	25—22	9—6	24—19
5—14	15—19 E	10—15	15—24
24—20 C	22—17	6—2	2—7
6—10	4—8	24—28	3—10
20—11	16—12	26—22	14—7 F
8—24	8—11	14—18	
28—19	17—13	22—17	Drawn

Notes by TOMMIE WISWELL

A A fairly even three mover, neither side having a preponderance of strength as in many openings under this style of play.

B Becoming more popular than 16—20 and would be my preference at this point. 9—13, 23—19, 10—14, 27—23, 11—16 same.

C These moves set the tempo of the game and should be noted by the student. It is the decisions a player makes early in the opening which decide whether or not he will have all "uphill" work or "easy sailing" in the middle and end game. Usually a weak end game or loss can be traced directly to poor judgment in the initial stages of the game.

D Black decides to launch a direct attack on the vulnerable White man on 19. It is usually good Checkers to locate your opponents weak spots and keep pressure on same—just as in war—the best defense is a good attack.

E If 4—8 the shot via 21—17, 14—21, 30—25, 21—30, 31—27, 30—23, 27—2, 10—14, 32—27 etc., draws.

F An interesting and keenly contested game which was highly enjoyed by all the spectators.

Variation 1

19—15 A	20—27	25—22	2—9
10—19	32—16	14—18	26—23
24—15	8—11	31—27	8—12
16—20	15—8	18—25	21—17
26—23	4—20	29—22	12—16
12—16	18—15	3—8	17—14
23—18	1—6	27—23	11—15
16—19	22—18	7—11	*Drawn*
30—26	9—14 B	23—18	
6—9	18—9	6—10	J. Alexander
27—24	5—14	15—6	

A 26—23 C, 16—20, 30—26, 8—11, 19—16, 12—19, 24—8, 4—11, 23—19, 5—9 D, 27—23, 9—14, 22—17, 13—22, 25—9, 6—13, 29—25, 10—14, 25—22, 7—10, 22—18, 1—5, 18—9, 5—14, 26—22, 11—15, 32—27, 15—24, 28—19, 2—7 E, 22—18, 14—17, 21—14, 10—17 etc. *Drawn*

B 3—8, 26—22, 8—12, 28—24 would also draw.

C A favorite line of Asa Long, the famous Toledo Master.

D Though this is safe enough Mr. Long is of the opinion that 6—9 might be a good substitute.

E Ward played 3—7 here against Long in the 1927 International Match and eventually came to grief. Text is much better and leads to an easy draw.

GAME 10

9—13, 23—19, 11—16

BLACK: Kenneth Grover		WHITE: J. B. Hanson	
9—13	8—11	6—9	14—18
23—19	19—16	23—19	22—15
11—16	12—19	9—13	7—11
27—23	24—8	27—23	15—8
10—14 *Var. 1*	4—11	11—15	3—19
22—17	25—22	30—26	21—17
13—22	7—10	15—24	13—22
25—9	22—18 *B*	28—19	26—17
5—14	1—5	2—7 *C*	19—23
29—25 *A*	18—9	19—15	17—14 *C*
16—20	5—14	10—19	
32—27	26—22	23—16	*Drawn*

Notes by TOMMIE WISWELL

A Varies from the preceding game and also leads to a sound line. However, I prefer 24—20.

B 23—19, 6—9, 22—17 would be another good way of playing it at this point.

C Note the similarity with note *A*, Variation 1, of previous game.

Variation 1

16-20	26-23	3-10	31-22
32-27	9-18	29-25	10-15
8-11	23-14	10-14	19-10
19-16	1-6	26-23	11-16
12-19	30-26	2-6	*Drawn*
24-8	6-9	28-24	
4-11	22-18	6-10	
23-18A	15-22	24-19	Nathan Rubin
10-15	25-18	13-17	
18-14B	7-10	25-22	
6-9	14-7	17-26	

A Varies from most published play and is very strong.

B 26-23, 7-10, 30-26, 5-9, 18-14, 9-18, 23-7, 3-10, 26-23, 6-9, 23-19C, 15-24, 28-19, 1-5, 19-16, 10-14, 16-7, 2-11, 31-26, 11-15, 26-23, 14-18, 23-14, 9-18, 21-17, 15-19, 22-15, 13-22, 25-18, 19-23, *Drawn*—J. C. Brown Vs. W. Miller.

C 27-24, 20-27, 31-24, 10-14, 24-20, 1-5, 23-19, 15-24, 28-19, 2-6, 19-16, 6-10, 16-7, 14-17, 21-14, 10-26. *Drawn* —Abe Herman.

GAME 11

11—16, 24—19, 7—11

BLACK: Kenneth Grover		WHITE: J. B. Hanson	
11—16	6—10	6—10	22—26
24—19	25—21	23—18	7—11
7—11 A	10—17	10—17	26—30
22—18	21—14	3—10	27—24
3—7 B	1—6	22—26	30—26
25—22	26—22 G	31—22	11—15
11—15 C	6—10 H	17—26	26—22
18—11	22—18	10—14	24—19
8—24	10—17	26—30	22—17
28—19	19—15	18—15	15—10
4—8	16—19	30—25	17—13
22—18 D	15—8	15—10	10—6
8—11 E	19—26	25—21	13—17
29—25	30—23	10—7	6—10 J
9—13—Var. 1	17—22	13—17	
18—14 F	18—14	7—3	Drawn
10—17	2—6 H	17—22	
21—14	8—3	3—7	

57

Notes by TOMMIE WISWELL

A The early moving of this "apex" piece to 11 creates a weakness which makes Black's game hard to handle. However, it remains quite drawable and has figured in several important encounters, including the Long-Hunt World's Title Match. (11–16, 22–18, 7–11, 24–19, same at next move.)

B Essential in this type of formation. In many of the three-movers Black's tasks consist largely in overcoming the initial weakness inherent in the opening moves and getting something approaching an equal game. In order to achieve this the second player *must* understand the idea behind the drawing theme. Guesswork will only prove fatal.

C The reason for Black's 3–7 move at Note *B*.

D 29–25, 8–11, 22–18, 9–13, 26–22, 6–9, 18–15, 11–18, 22–6, 1–10, 25–22, 9–14, 22–18, 7–11, 18–9, 5–14, 30–25, 2–7, 25–22, 14–17, 21–14, 10–26, 31–22, 16–20, 22–18, 11–16, 32–28, 13–17, 19–15, 16–19, 23–16, 12–19, 18–14, 17–22, 14–9, 22–25, 9–5, 25–30, 5–1, 30–25, 1–6, 25–22, is a variation played between Ray Cast and Barney Talis.

E 9–13 can also be played now.

F Varies from Note *D* and leads to a fine original ending.

G Willie Ryan shows the following play at this point: 23–18, 16–23, 26–19, 6–10, 27–24, 10–17, 19–15, 11–16, 24–20, 17–22, 20–11, 7–16, 15–11, 13–17, 11–8, 16–19, 8–3, 5–9, 18–15, 9–13, 3–8, 19–23, 31–27, etc. *Drawn*

H From this stage to the end, Mr. Grover plays good crossboard checkers and manoeuvers his pieces to a well-earned draw.

I White tried hard to score, but Black's stonewall defense proved impregnable.

Variation 1

9–14	1–5	14–21	6–10	10–14	25–29
18–9	18–9	23–18	3–8	15–10	1–5
5–14	5–14	12–16	23–27	9–13	29–25
25–22	26–22	19–12	8–11	10–6	5–9
11–15	16–20	15–19	27–31	14–17	25–22
32–28	27–24	24–15	11–16	22–18	18–14
15–24	20–27	10–19	2–6	17–22	22–17
28–19	31–24	12–8	16–19	19–24	14–10
7–11	11–15	19–23	6–9	22–25	17–22
22–18	21–17	8–3	18–15	6–1	9–14,

and 31–26, 30–23, 22–18. *Drawn*

GAME 12

11–16, 24–19, 7–11

BLACK: J. B. Hanson		WHITE: Kenneth Grover	
11–16	19–15	23–26	27–24
24–19	11–18^D	14–9	29–25
7–11	22–6	7–10	31–27
22–18	1–10	1–6	25–18
3–7	25–22	10–14	23–14
25–22–$Var.1$	14–17	6–10	30–26
11–15	21–14	14–17	6–10
18–11	10–17	10–14	26–31
8–24	23–18	17–21	10–7
28–19	17–21	14–18	16–19
4–8	18–14	26–30	24–15
22–18	21–25	18–23	31–24
8–11	14–9	21–25	7–11
29–25	25–30	9–5	24–20
9–13	9–5	2–7	14–18
25–22	30–23	5–1	13–17
6–9	27–18	7–11	15–10
30–25^A	16–19	32–27	20–24
9–14^B	5–1	25–29	11–15
18–9	19–23	1–6	17–21
5–14^C	18–14	11–16	18–23

60

21—25	7—11	28—32	27—32
10—7	24—28	11—15	28—24
25—30	15—19	22—17	23—18
7—2	28—32	15—18	24—19
30—25	19—24	17—21	32—28
2—7	32—28	18—22	12—16
25—22	24—27	32—28 E	28—32

and continue: 16—20, 22—26, 21—25, 32—28, 25—21, 26—22, 20—24, 22—26, 24—27, 28—32, 27—31, 26—22, 19—23, 18—27, 31—24. *Drawn*

Notes by TOMMIE WISWELL

A A deceiving sacrifice here is 19—15, 10—19, 30—25 but 19—24, 27—20, 7—10 takes all the sting out of the White game and puts the shoe on the other foot. See Variation 2 for a likely continuation.

B Edwin F. Hunt is the author of the following nice variation: 10—14, 27—24, 7—10, 24—20, 2—6, 18—15, 11—27, 20—11, 10—15, 31—24, 14—17, 21—14, 9—18, 19—10, 6—15, 24—19, 15—24, 22—15, 5—9, 15—10, 13—17, 25—21, 1—5, 21—14, 9—18. *Drawn*

This is more generally known that Mr. Hanson's 9—14 in the above game which brought the game into new territory.

C And we arrive at the following interesting position.

BLACK (Hanson) 1, 2, 7, 10, 11, 12, 13, 14, 16

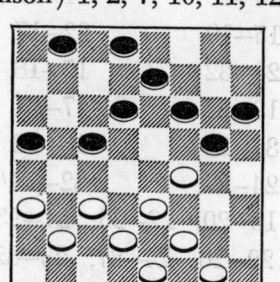

WHITE (Grover) 19, 21, 22, 23, 25, 26, 27, 31, 32

White to Play

D The correct jump 10–19 would simply be "fishing in troubled waters." A probable continuation on this exchange would be: 10–19, 22–18, 7–10 (1–5, 18–9, 5–14, 25–22, *White wins*) 18–9, 11–15, 9–5, 10–14, 25–22, 13–17, 22–13, 2–6, 32–28, 15–18, 21–17, 14–21, 23–14, 21–25, 27–24, 25–30, 24–15, 30–23, 14–9, 23–18, 9–2, 18–11, 28–24 or 31–26. *White wins*—Tommie Wiswell.

E Black's position looks dubious but actually we now have a published draw. Never-the-less, Mr. Hanson was forced to make numerous star moves.

Variation 1

28–24 at this stage was introduced by Edwin F. Hunt, former United States Champion, in his World's title match with Asa Long in 1936.

28–24	5–9	23–16	10–15
16–20	29–25	12–19	18–11
25–22 A	8–11	32–16	14–17
11–15	25–22	6–10	*Drawn*
18–11	11–16	16–11	
8–15	27–23	10–14	
23–18 B	20–27	26–23	
9–13 C	31–24	1–5	
18–11	16–20	11–8	
7–23	30–26	2–6	
26–19	20–27	8–3	
4–8	19–15	6–10	
22–18	10–19	3–8	

A There is no future for White in 18–14 as the following will show: 18–14, 9–18, 23–14, 10–17, 21–14, 6–9, 26–23, 9–18, 23–14, 11–16, 31–26, 16–23, 26–19, 8–11, 30–26, 1–6, 25–22, 11–16, 26–23, 6–10, 22–17, 2–6, 29–25, 4–8, 25–22, 6–9, 22–18, 9–13, 18–15, 13–22, 15–6, 7–11, 14–10, 22–26, 19–15. *Drawn*—Nathan Rubin.

B A very fine move which forces Black to play with care. It was good enough to defeat Long and reflects great credit on Mr. Hunt.

C Long played 7–11 here and lost as follows: 7–11, 29–25, 1–14 D, 19–10, 6–15, 27–23 E, 20–27, 31–24, 12–16, 21–17, 14–21, 23–19, 16–23, 26–10, 11–16, 18–14, 9–18, 22–15, 16–19, 24–20, 19–23, 25–22, 5–9, 22–18, 9–13, 15–11, 13–17, 10–7, 23–26, 30–23, 21–25, 7–3, 25–30, 23–19, 30–26, 19–15, 26–22, 32–28, 17–21, 28–24, 21–25, 24–19, 25–30, 19–16, 30–26, 11–7, 2–11, 16–7, 26–23, 7–2, 23–14, 15–10, 14–7, 3–10, 22–17, 20–16, 17–13, 2–7, 1–5, 10–6, 13–17, 16–12, 17–13, 12–8, 4–11, 7–16, 5–9, 16–19, 9–14, 19–23. *White wins*

D Mr. Rubin shows that 9–14 here also loses: 9–14, 18–9, 5–14, 22–17, 4–8, 26–23, 11–16, 25–22, 8–11, 17–13, 6–9, 13–6, 2–9, 22–17, 9–13, 30–26, 13–22, 26–17, 15–18, 17–13, 18–22, 13–9, 22–25, 9–6, 25–30, 6–2, 30–25, 2–6, 11–15, 6–9, 15–18, 21–17. *White wins*

E Mr. Hunt played well here as the following shows: 24–19, 15–24, 18–15, 11–18, 22–15, 4–8, 15–10, 12–16, 25–22, 8–12, 26–23, 9–13, 30–26, 16–19, 23–16, 12–19, 10–7, 2–11, 22–17, 13–22, 26–10, 11–15, 10–7, 15–18, 27–23, 18–27, 32–16, 24–27. *Drawn*–Rubin.

Variation 2

The following appears to correct published play which gives 19–15 as a loss.

19–15	11–15	21–14	17–21
10–19	20–11	23–18	18–22
30–25 *A*	15–24 *E*	7–2	24–27
19–24 *B*	10–7	18–9	14–18
27–20	24–27	13–6	27–32
7–10	7–3	1–10	18–23
31–27 *C*	27–31	8–11	5–9
10–15	3–8	10–14	23–18
21–17	2–6 *F*	11–15	32–27
9–14 *D*	11–7	12–16	22–17
17–10	31–27 *G*	2–6	9–13
13–17	23–18	16–20	17–22
22–13	6–10	6–10	*Drawn*
15–31	25–21	14–17	
32–28	27–23	15–18	Tommie
31–24	18–14	20–24	Wiswell
28–19	10–17	10–14	

64

A In a New York Masters Tourney some years back Milton Loew played 32–28 here and lost ingloriously as follows: 32–28, 7–10, 27–24, 10–15, 22–17?, 13–22, 26–17, 19–26. *Black won*

B The move that takes all the sting out of the White game and puts the shoe on the other foot.

C 32–28 *H*, 1–6, 31–27, 9–14, 18–9, 5–14, 27–24, (22–18, 6–9, 18–15, 11–18, 20–11, 13–17. *Black wins*) 10–15, 24–19, 15–24, 28–19, 13–17, 22–13, 14–18, 23–14, 16–30, 14–9, 11–15, 9–5, 15–18, 5–1, 6–9, 13–6, 2–9, 1–6, 9–13, 6–10, 30–26, 10–15, 26–22, 21–17, 22–29, 15–22, 29–25, 22–29, 13–22. *Black wins*

D Otherwise White plays 32–28 on his next move and has the situation well in hand.

E Black's position appears strong but White manages to squeeze through for a man down draw.

F The Black King is temporarily neutralized and Black has nothing better at the moment. If 31–27 or 31–26 White plays 25–21, 27–18, 11–7 and it is Black who has to look for the draw.

G 31–26, 23–19 and Black can go no further.

H The 2nd National Tourney book (page 167) shows 32–27, 10–15, 18–14, 9–18, 23–14, 2–7. *Black wins* (George Bass *vs.* Hubert Dunn). However, the annotator makes no mention of 31–27 at Note *C* of the above trunk.

GAME 13

9—13, 23—18, 10—15

BLACK: J. B. Hanson		WHITE: Kenneth Grover	
9—13	11—18	8—12	2—6
23—18	26—22 E	16—11	11—7
10—15 A	12—16 F	17—21	4—8
27—23 B	22—15	25—22	19—15
6—10	7—10	6—10	12—16
32—27	14—7	22—17	7—3
1—6 C	3—26	10—15 H	19—15
18—14	30—23	23—19	8—12
10—17	16—20 G	15—24	3—7
21—14	24—19	28—19	W. Wins
15—18 D	13—17	5—9	
22—15	19—16	17—13	

Notes by J. B. HANSON

A A weak three-mover, White having the attack on most of the variations.

B 18—14 is another strong attack but is met by 6—9, 26—23, 9—18, 23—14 and now 12—16 will draw with careful play.

C Many of the experts favor 5—9 here.

D The only good move here as White is playing for a trap by 14—10, 7—14, 22—18. *White wins*

E Strong. Black must play with care.

F Best by a long shot. 7—11 is weak, if not a loss, therefore let your opponent play it.

G Ryan's Encyclopedia plays 6—10 here but I think 16—20 is equally as good. If 13—17, White wins by a fancy trap— 25—21, 17—22, 31—26, 22—31, 24—20, 31—24, 28—3. *White wins.* After 6—10, 25—21, 16—20, 24—19, 8—12, 23—18, 10—14, 18—9, 5—14, 19—15, 4—8, 27—23, 12—16 (If 2—6, 28—24, 20—27, 31—24, 13—17, 29—25, *White wins*) 29—25, 2—6, 25—22, 8—12, 15—11, 16—19, 23—16, 12—19, 11—7, 6—10, 7—3, 10—15, 3—7, 14—18, 7—11, 18—25, 11—18, 25—30, 18—15, 19—23, 28—24, 20—27, 31—24. *Drawn*

H Loses, as White has the move on all the pieces. We diagram the position after 12—16 instead, which would lead to a pretty draw:

BLACK (Hanson) 2, 4, 5, 10, 16, 20, 21

WHITE (Grover) 11, 17, 23, 27, 28, 29, 31

White to Play

Continue:

31—26, (best) 10—15, 17—13, 2—6, 11—7, 4—8, 23—18, (nothing better, if 7—3, 6—10, 3—19, 15—31 *Black wins*) 15—31, 7—2, 31—24, 28—3, 20—24, 2—9, 5—14. *Drawn*

GAME 14

9—13, 23—18, 10—15

BLACK: Kenneth Grover   WHITE: J. B. Hanson

9—13	11—18	17—22	6—9
23—18	26—22	19—16	11—7
10—15	12—16	8—12 D	4—8
27—23	22—15	16—11	7—3
6—10	7—10	5—9	8—11 F
32—27	14—7	21—17	29—25
1—6 A—Var. 1	3—26	9—13	22—29
18—14	30—23	28—24	3—8
10—17	16—20 C	6—10	13—22
21—14	24—19	24—19	8—13
15—18	13—17	2—6	29—25
22—15	25—21	23—18	White wins

Notes by J. B. HANSON

A Mr. Grover adopts the same defense. 5—9 is probably easier to handle than the more usual 1—6 continuation and may become popular in future matches.

B Corrects Master Play where 8—12, 27—24, etc. *White wins*
C Safe enough.

D There does not seem to be a draw for Black now. Instead 6—10, 16—12 E, 8—11, 12—8, 11—16, 8—3, 5—9, 23—18, 10—14, 18—15, 16—19. *Drawn*

68

E If 23—19, 5—9, 16—12, 8—11, 12—8, 11—15, 8—3, 15—24, 28—19, 9—14, 19—16, 10—15, 16—11, 14—18, 3—7, 22—25, 29—22, 18—25, 27—23, 4—8, 11—4, 2—11, 4—8, 11—16, 8—12, 15—19. *Drawn*

F By making this move Mr. Grover allowed a shot for the benefit of the spectators.

Variation 1

5—9	22—15	1—6	31—26
18—14	11—18	23—19	7—11
9—18	20—11	15—24	19—15
23—14	8—15	28—19	13—17
10—17	26—22	3—8	25—22
21—14	4—8	22—15	18—25
12—16	30—26	6—10	29—13
24—20	8—12	15—6	11—18
15—18 *B*	26—23	2—18	*Drawn*

69

GAME 15

12—16, 23—18, 16—20

BLACK: Kenneth Grover		WHITE: J. B. Hanson	
12—16	31—22	26—23	28—24
23—18	7—10	17—13	7—11
16—20 A	23—19	2—7	1—5
26—23 B	11—16	10—6	22—26
8—12—Var. 1	19—15	1—10	32—28
30—26	10—19	9—6	3—8
9—14 C	24—15	10—14	21—17 F
18—9	16—19	25—21	11—16
5—14	18—14	14—18	20—11
22—18 D	20—24	6—1	8—15
14—17	27—20	18—22	17—13
21—14	19—23	1—6	23—18
10—17	22—17	22—26	5—9
25—21	23—26	13—9	15—19
6—10	15—10	26—30	24—15
21—14	26—30	9—5	18—11
10—17	14—9	30—26	
26—22 E	30—26	5—1	Drawn
17—26	29—25	26—22	

Notes by J. B. HANSON

A A pretty opening, slightly in favor of White.

B As good as there is.

C Although 10—14 is usually played here I believe the text is best.

70

D 22—17 is tricky—hoping for 4—8, 26—22 and we have the famous "Dunne's Win." It goes as follows: 11—16, 24—19, 8—11, 22—18, 1—5, 18—9, 6—22, 25—18, 10—14, 18—9, 5—14, 29—25, 7—10, 25—22, 11—15, 23—18, 15—24, 18—9, 10—14, 28—19, 16—23, 27—18, 14—23, 22—18, 12—16, 21—17, 16—19, 32—28, 20—24, 17—13, 23—27, 9—6, 2—9, 13—6, 27—32, 6—2, 32—27, 18—15, 27—23, 2—7. *White wins*

E 24—19 leads to some very pretty play, 17—21, 18—15, 11—18, 23—14, 4—8, 27—23, 8—11, 23—18, 20—24, 26—23, 11—15, 18—11, 7—16, 32—27, 16—20, 19—15, 1—6, 28—19, 21—25, 29—22, 6—10, 14—7, 2—25.—J. Alexander

F 6—10 would be very weak here, if not an actual loss by 11—16, 20—11, 8—15, 10—19, 23—16, etc.

Variation 1

11—15 is also good here and was a favorite of James Ferrie, once Champion of the World.

11—15	18—9	11—15	26—17
18—11	5—14	29—25	19—26
8—15	25—22	15—19	31—22
24—19	11—15	25—22	10—15
15—24	32—28	6—9	17—10
28—19	15—24	17—13	7—14
4—8	28—19	10—15	27—23
22—18	7—11	13—6	*Drawn*
8—11	19—16	1—10	
30—26	2—7	22—18	
9—14	22—17	15—22	

71

GAME 16

12–16, 23–18, 16–20

BLACK: J. B. Hanson WHITE: Kenneth Grover

12–16	17–13*E*	10–17	18–9
23–18	3–7	3–10	5–14
16–20	31–26	6–31	32–27
24–19*A*	12–16*K*	13–6	2–6
10–14*B*	19–12	31–24	19–16
26–23*C*	4–8	28–19	6–9
8–12	12–3	1–10	16–7
22–17	14–17	23–18	17–22
7–10*D*	21–14	10–14	25–18

and 14–32, 7–2*L*, *Drawn*

Notes by J. B. HANSON

A Varies from the preceding game and is equally as good. It plays for 8–12, an early loss by 19–15, 10–19, 18–14, 9–18, 22–8, 4–11, 27–24, 20–27, 31–8. *White wins.* One of the most natural losses on the Checker board and has caused thousands of novices to come to grief.

B Undoubtedly the best move at this point.

C Forces the Bristol-Cross, White having slightly the better of it.

D 11–16 is weak and should be avoided.

E 30–26, 11–16*F*, 26–22, 9–13, 18–9, 5–14, 22–18, 13–22,

18–9, 6–13, 25–18, **4–8**G, 29–25H, 8–11, 18–15, 11–18,
23–7, 3–10, 25–22, 16–23, 27–18, 1–5J, 32–27, 2–7, 18–15,
10–19, 27–24, 20–27, 31–15. *Drawn*

F 4–8 is bad. Richard Jordan beat James Wyllie as follows:
19–15, 10–19, 17–10, 6–22, 23–7, 3–10, 25–18, 9–14, 18–9,
5–14, 29–25, 10–15, 26–22, 1–6, 22–17, 6–10, 17–13, 2–6,
21–17, 14–30, 31–26, 30–23, 27–4, 10–14, 4–8, 14–17, 8–11
6–10, 11–7, 10–15, 7–10, 15–19, 32–27, 17–22, 10–15. *White
wins*

G George Buchanan's improvement, easier than 2–6.

H 18–15, 1–6, 29–25, 3–7, 31–26, 13–17, 21–14, 10–17,
28–24, 7–11, 15–10, 6–15, 19–10, 17–21, 25–22, 11–15.
Black should win—Alexander.

J R. Stewart played 12–16 against Richard Jordan for the
World's title in 1897. The move loses by 32–27, 2–7, 27–23,
1–5, 31–27, 7–11, 28–24, 5–9, 24–19. *White wins*

K Star move and forces simple end play. 11–16 loses as
follows: 11–16, 25–22, 14–17, 21–14, 10–17, 29–25, 17–21,
19–15, 7–10, 15–11, 10–15, 11–7, 2–11, 28–24, 4–8, 32–28,
etc. *White wins*

L Both players found it advisable to stick to the "straight
and narrow" and not take any unnecessary risks.

GAME 17

9—14, 24—19, 5—9

BLACK: J. B. Hanson		WHITE: Kenneth Grover	
9—14	7—11	14—17	11—27
24—19	25—22 *B*	21—14	18—2
5—9 *A*	1—5 *C*	10—17	27—32
22—18	27—24	19—16 *K*	2—6
11—15—*Var. 1*	16—20	12—19	32—27
18—11	32—28	23—16	6—9
8—24	20—27	17—22	27—23
28—19	31—24	26—17	9—14
4—8	9—13 *E*	13—22	22—26
25—22	18—9	28—24	30—25
8—11	5—14	6—10	26—30
22—18	24—20 *G*	16—12	25—21
11—16	2—7 *H*	10—15	30—26 *M*
29—25	22—18	20—16 *L*	Drawn

Notes by J. B. HANSON

A Starts an equal game on most variations.

B 18—15 is another safe line.

C If 3—8 *D*, 27—24, 16—20, 32—28, 20—27, 31—24, 11—16, 19—15, 10—19, 24—15, 6—10, 15—6, 1—10, 18—15, 10—19, 22—17. *Drawn*

D 3—7, 32—28, 16—20, 21—17, 14—21, 19—15. *White wins*

74

E Stronger than 11—16, however, Black has a chance for a trap and many play it for this reason. 11—16, 19—15, 10—19, 24—15, 16—19, 23—16, 12—19, 26—23, 19—26, 30—23, 3—7, 28—24*F*, 9—13, 18—9, 5—14. *Black wins*

F 22—17, 7—10, 28—24. *Drawn*

G Mr. Grover makes the star move. If 22—18, 11—16, 18—9, 16—20, 9—5, 20—27, 5—1, 10—14, 1—17, 13—31. *Black wins*

H 11—15, 20—16, 15—24, 28—19, 14—18, 23—7*J*, 2—20, 19—15, 20—24, 21—17, 6—9, 26—23, 24—27, 23—18, 27—31, 17—14, 31—27, 14—5, 27—23, 18—14, 23—18, 14—10, 18—11, 5—1, 12—16, 1—5. *Drawn*—Reed *vs.* Barker

J 22—15, 13—17, 21—7, 2—27. *Black wins*

K Only move to draw. For other interesting play see GROVER and WISWELL'S "LET'S PLAY CHECKERS."

L Correct.

M We were both on solid ground all the way.

Variation 1

11—16*A*	28—19	3—8*C*	22—18
26—22	4—8	26—23	20—24
7—11	30—26	8—12	27—11
22—17	8—11	29—25	1—5
16—20*B*	19—16	11—16	23—16
17—13	12—19	32—28	14—30
11—15	23—7	10—15	25—22
18—11	2—11	31—26	12—19
8—24	25—22	15—19	*Drawn*

A A favorite line of the Brooklyn Master, Louis Ginsberg.

B Hoping for 30—26, 20—24, 27—20, 11—16, 20—11, 8—22, 25—18, 9—13, 18—9, 13—22, 26—17, 6—22. *Black wins.* It seems this is about all Black can play for in this line.

C 11—15 loses by 27—23, 3—8, 31—27, 8—12, 22—17, 15—18, 29—25, 12—16, 26—22, 16—19, 23—16, 18—23, 27—18, 14—23, 16—11, 23—26, 11—7, 26—31, 7—2, 31—26, 17—14. *White wins—* J. Alexander

GAME 18

9-14, 24-19, 5-9

BLACK: Kenneth Grover	WHITE: J. B. Hanson		
9-14	21-17	11-15	27-24
24-19	14-21	30-26	12-16
5-9	23-5	21-25	24-20
22-18	16-23	26-22	16-19
11-15	26-19-Var. 1	25-30	20-16
18-11	3-8B-Var. 2	23-18	11-20
8-24	27-23	30-25	2-7
28-19	8-11	18-11	20-16
4-8	32-28	25-18	13-9
25-22	6-9	11-7	19-23
8-11	25-22	10-15	9-6
22-18	2-6G	19-10	1-10
11-16	28-24	6-15	7-14
29-25	9-13	7-2	23-27
7-11	31-27D	15-19	5-1
18-15A	13-17G	24-15	27-32H
11-18	22-13	18-11	Drawn

Notes by J. B. HANSON

A Varies from the preceding game and is a standard line that has stood the test of time.

B Mr. Grover varies here. 3–7 is usually played, 25–22, 7–11, 27–23 *E*, 6–9, 32–28, 11–16, 22–18, 9–13, 28–24 *F*, 16–20, 18–15, 20–27, 15–6, 2–9, 31–24, 21–25. *Drawn*

C Or 11–16, which would have run into a now famous Ferrie-Jordan variation.

D If 31–26, 6–9, 22–18, 13–17, 24–20, 12–16, 19–12, 10–15, 20–16, 15–31, 16–7, 21–25, 30–14, 9–27. *Drawn*

E Here is a pretty stroke: 31–26, 11–15, 27–24, 2–7, 24–20, 15–24, 30–25, 21–30, 32–28, 30–23, 28–19, 23–16, 20–2. *Drawn*

F 18–15 loses by a beautiful shot: 21–25, 30–21, 13–17, 15–6, 2–9, 21–14, 9–27. *Black wins.* Ferrie beat Bonar on this ending many years ago.

G An interesting position, worthy of a diagram.

The setting at Note *G*:

BLACK (Grover) 1, 6, 10, 11, 12, 13, 21

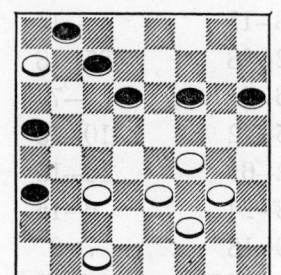

WHITE (Hanson) 5, 19, 22, 23, 24, 27, 30

Black to Play

Continue from note *G* of trunk.

H A most interesting game, especially from note *C* on.

Variation 1

27–18 A	18–14	31–26	14–9
12–16	13–22	15–18	6–13
25–22 B	14–7	17–14	26–23
6–9	3–10	16–19	19–26
22–17	26–17	32–27	30–14
9–13	10–15	2–6	*Drawn*
			J. Alexander

A This 27–18 take is inferior, but quite drawable.

B If now 26–23, 2–7, 32–27, 7–11, 25–22, 6–9, 27–24, 16–20, 31–27, 3–8, 24–19, 8–12, 22–17, 9–13, 18–15, 13–22, 15–8, 10–14. *Back wins*

Variation 2

2–7	32–28	6–15	14–10
25–22	15–24	23–18	12–16
7–11	28–19	15–19	22–18
27–23	10–15	18–14	16–20
11–15	19–10	19–24	10–6 *Drawn*

GAME 19

11—16, 22—17, 7—11

BLACK: Kenneth Grover		WHITE: J. B. Hanson	
11—16	3—8 *D*	1—5	15—19
22—17	18—9	29—25	14—9
7—11 *A*	5—14	5—14	19—23
24—19 *B*	26—22	25—22	9—5
9—14	11—15	4—8	6—10
25—22	30—25	31—27	5—1
11—15	15—24	8—11	10—15
17—13	27—11	23—18 *G*	13—9
15—24	8—15	14—23	15—19 *H*
28—19	22—18 *E*	27—18	
8—11	15—22	10—15	*Drawn*
22—18 *C*	25—9	18—14	

Notes by WILLIAM F. RYAN

A A somewhat tough three-mover for Black, but it can be made to appear more difficult than it really is if the principal drawing lines are not known.

B The text offers White little more than an even game, and is generally considered inferior to 17—14 as taken in the next game. It is surprising how many of our leading players are not yet thoroughly groomed on the basic lines of play following this move, as covered in Notes *C, D, and E*.

80

C Equally good is 29—25, 11—15* (the only move to draw!), 22—17, 15—24, 27—11, 3—7 (3—8 also draws, but it is no sleigh ride), 25—22, 7—16, 23—19, 16—23, 26—19, 4—8, 30—26, 8—11, 26—23, 5—9*, 31—26, 11—15*, 32—28, 15—24, 28—19, 10—15*!, 19—10, 6—15, 17—10, 9—14, 13—9, 12—16*, 9—5, 16—20*, 22—17, 2—6*, 26—22, 14—18*, 23—14, 6—9. *Drawn*—Wm. F. Ryan Vs. Nathan Rubin. Known as Strickland's Draw.

D Very weak, and was once published to lose. The proper route is: 3—7, 18—9, 5—14, 29—25, 11—15 (now a well known Pioneer landing), 25—22, 15—24, 27—11, 7—16, 22—18 (if 31—27, 16—19 draws), 1—5, 18—9, 5—14, 26—22, 16—19, 23—16, 12—19, 22—17, 4—8, 32—27, 2—7*, 27—23, 19—26, 30—23, 7—11, 31—27, 11—16*, 27—24, 16—20, 24—19, 8—12. *Drawn*—Published Play.

E Mr. Hanson here passed up his chance to put on the heat by: 13—9!, 6—13, 22—17, 13—22, 25—11, 10—15, 29—25, 15—19*F*, 23—16, 12—19, 32—27, 1—6, 25—22, 6—9, 31—26, 9—13, 27—23, 19—24, 22—18, 14—17, 21—14, 24—27, 23—19, 27—31, 26—23, 31—26, 18—15, 26—22, 23—18, 22—17, etc. *Drawn.* This play was published under my name as Game No. 24 in my American Checkerist magazine.

F After showing the draw in Note *E*, Frank Miller of Seattle pointed out an alternative draw here by: 15—18, 32—27, 12—16*, 31—26, 16—20*, 23—19, 20—24*, 27—20, 18—23, 26—22, 23—26, 19—16, 26—30, 22—17, 14—18, 17—13, 30—26, 21—17, 26—23.* *Drawn*

G The situation has now reduced itself to one of marked simplicity, and the draw becomes imminent.

H Nothing has been missed, but Jesse could have worked his pieces to greater advantage at Note *E*. There is no gainsaying, of course, that he might have won.

GAME 20

11–16, 22–17, 7–11

BLACK: J. B. Hanson		WHITE: Kenneth Grover	
11–16	1–6	10–17	22–26
22–17	23–14	21–14	11–8
7–11	15–18	2–6	26–30
17–14 A	17–13	27–24 G	8–3
10–17	16–20	20–27	30–26
21–14	24–19	31–24	3–8
9–18	8–11	18–27	26–22
23–14	19–15	32–23	8–11
11–15 B	12–16	16–19	22–18
25–22	15–8	23–16	11–7
3–7	4–11	15–18	18–9
29–25	30–26	24–20	7–2
6–9 C	11–15	18–22	6–10
22–17	26–23	16–11	13–6
9–18	6–10	7–16	10–15
26–23	25–21	20–11	*White wins*

Notes by WILLIAM F. RYAN

A Varies from the preceding game and is the oyster of the
opening. Mr. Grover has done very well with this attack. He
turned the tide in this match with it, and at the 10th A.C.A.
tourney in 1939 he defeated the redoubtable Asa Long with
the same line. If a player is exceedingly well grounded in some

82

openings, it will help to make up any deficiencies he may show on other openings. Mr. Grover may not be equally adept on all the 3-movers (who is?) but he is a specialist, and when on his own territory is a formidable opponent. See Game 3, Variation 1 for further play

B 6–9 and 3–7 also draw, but both lines are very critical and best avoided. The text is best and leads to a good draw.

C A probable loss. The proper and only move to draw is 16–19, and the best attack against it was first published in the 1940 edition of my Modern Encyclopedia of Checkers, to improve a game played between Edwin F. Hunt and H. B. Reynolds. The following play is taken from the 1940 edition of my Modern Encyclopedia of Checkers, and shows how carefully Black must handle his mid game to land a draw:

16–19*	30–14	11–18	26–23	6–15 F
25–21	7–11	31–26 E	18–22	Drawn
6–9*	14–9 D	12–16*	28–24	Wm. F. Ryan
22–17	5–14	21–17	16–20	
9–18	17–10	8–11*	23–18	
26–23	15–19	17–13	2–6	
19–26	24–15	11–15	18–11	

D 24–19, 15–24, 28–19, 1–6, is easy for Black. If 27–23, then 11–16, 14–9, 5–14, 17–10, 16–19, 23–16, 12–19, 31–26, 8–12, 21–17, 4–8*, 17–13 (32–27, 12–16*), 2–6*, 32–27, 15–18*!, 24–15, 18–23, 26–19, 8–11. Drawn

E 27–23, 18–27, 32–23, 8–11, 28–24, 11–15, 21–17 4–8, 17–13, 8–11, 24–20, 2–6, 10–7 (31–26, 11–16, 20–11, 15–19, 23–16, 6–15, Drawn), 15–19, 23–16, 12–19, 7–3, 11–15, 3–7, 15–18, 7–11, 18–22, 11–15, 19–24, 15–18, 22–25, 18–14, 25–30, 20–16, 30–25, 16–11, 24–28, 11–8, 28–32, 8–3, 1–5,

3–8, 32–28, 31–27, 25–22, 8–11, 22–26, *Drawn*–Joint analysis by Walter Hallman and Wm. F. Ryan. At the Cedar Point, Ohio, Master's Tournament in 1938, I showed Mr. Hallman the play in Notes C and D. We then went over the line together and produced the supplementary attack shown in this note.

F It is impossible to scientifically draw the 11–16, 22–17, 7–11, opening, without knowledge of the play shown in Notes C, D, and E, as the tenability of Black's defense virtually hinges on it.

G The crusher, and wins at once. The win looks very familiar, but I cannot recall where I have seen it before, but I am sure that it has been shown or played prior to this match. Grover has forced the win with masterly finesse.

GAME 21

9–14, 23–19, 14–18

BLACK: J. B. Hanson WHITE: Kenneth Grover

9–14	10–14	10–15	30–25
23–19	29–25 F	17–10	11–7
14–18 A	5–9	7–14	3–10
22–15	27–23 G	20–16	14–7
11–18	18–27	8–12	25–22
26–22 B	32–23	16–11	17–13
7–11	11–15 H	12–16	19–23
22–15	19–10	30–26	7–2
11–18	6–15	14–18	15–18
21–17	13–6	21–17	2–7
2–7 E	1–10	18–23	16–20
17–13	25–22 K	26–22	28–24
8–11	15–19	23–26	
24–20 F	23–16	17–14	*Drawn*
4–8	12–19	26–30	
25–21 F	22–17 S	22–17	

Notes by WILLIAM F. RYAN

A Comparatively little attention has been focused upon this colorful three-mover, though it is by no means lacking in depth. A number of excellent games have already been played on it by leading experts, and these have enabled the champions to gage the opening's ramifications with reasonable accuracy. It appears that White gains the "pull," or "initiative,"

on most variations, but of course such advantages as may be obtained are not of the same force so evident in some of the more critical three-movers.

B This continues to remain the favorite attack with heavy-weight players, on the presumption that the run-off weakens Black's structure more than it does White. An overall examination of games contested on the text move seems to justify its favorable rating.

Another good move here for White is 26—23, though it does not offer as much variety or strength as 26—22. The following outlines all the salient points of the 26—23 line:

Judd L. Palmer vs. F. M. Wolford

26—23	23—14	29—25	13—6	6—1
10—14 *C*	10—17	1—6	2—18	16—19
24—20	25—22	27—23	19—15	27—23
8—11	11—15	14—18	5—9	*Drawn*
28—24	22—13	23—14	15—10	
6—10	8—11	11—16	9—14	
31—26	19—10	20—11	10—6	
4—8 *D*	7—14	7—23	14—17	
21—17	24—19	26—19	32—27	
14—21	3—7	6—9	12—16	

C 8—11, 23—14, 10—17, 21—14, 6—9, is said to draw, but after 14—10, 7—14, 25—22*, 4—8, 29—25*, Black definitely has a hard game.

D Or 1—6, 21—17, 14—21, 23—14, 10—17, 25—22, 7—10, 22—13, 3—7, 27—23, 10—14, 29—25, 14—18, 23—14, 11—16, 20—11, 7—23, 26—19, 6—9, 13—6, 2—18, 32—27, 5—9, 24—20, 9—14, 19—15, 14—17, etc. *Drawn*—George Heinl vs. J. L. Palmer.

E With this move, Mr. Hanson breaks now ground. The text is off beaten paths as far as I know, but in view of the succeeding play it is no improvement on 8—11.

F Mr. Grover decides to bide time with a series of well timed waiting moves, pending further developments. White's strategy is noteworthy.

G The only move to draw, and Kenneth was not to be caught napping! Black seems to be strongly arrayed at this point, but it is all a positional mirage, with White setting a fine trap by 27—23.

H Right into the net jumps Black. The text is the most natural move on the board, but it loses! The proper play is: 1—5, 31—27, 14—18*, 23—14, 9—18, 21—17, 7—10*J*, 25—21, 18—22*, 27—23, 22—25, 23—18, 25—29, 17—14, 10—17, 21—14, 6—10, 14—7, 3—10, 28—24, 10—14, etc. *Drawn*

J 6—10, 25—22, 18—25, 30—21, 10—14*, 17—10, 7—14, 13—9, 14—18, 9—6, 18—22, 6—2, 22—26, 27—24, 26—31, 21—17, is a hard ending for Black.

K This is where Grover missed his chance to corner his worthy adversary. The move taken only draws, but a win is to be had. See diagram:

BLACK (Hanson) 3, 7, 8, 10, 12, 14, 15

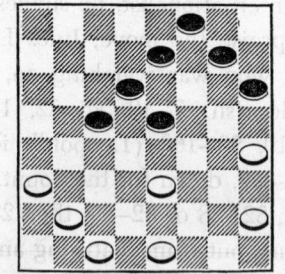

WHITE (Grover) 20, 21, 23, 25, 28, 30, 31

Proceed from diagram:

28–24*	19–10	6–1	16–11*!
15–18 L	23–30 O	30–25	12–16
31–27*	25–21	1–6	9–6*! R
8–11	11–15	25–22	16–20
30–26*	10–6 P	6–9*	6–10*!
10–15	15–19	22–18	*White wins*
23–19* M	24–15	21–17*	Wm. F. Ryan
14–17 N	7–10	18–15 Q	
21–14*	14–7	20–16*!	
18–23	3–19	15–18	

L 8–11, 30–26*, 12–16 (14–17, 21–14, 10–17, 25–21, 17–22, 26–17, 12–16, 17–14, 3–8, 14–9, 8–12, 9–6, 16–19, 23–16, 12–28, 6–2, 15–19, 21–17, 28–32, 17–14, 32–28, 2–6, etc. *White wins*), 25–22, 14–18, 23–14, 10–17, 21–14, 16–19, 14–9, 19–28, 26–23, 28–32, 9–6, 3–8, 6–2, 8–12, 2–6, 28–32, 23–18, 15–19, 18–14, *White wins*

M 26–22 only draws by 12–16*, 24–19 (22–17, 7–10, 17–13, 3–8, 13–9, 18–22, *draws*), 15–31, 22–8, 3–12, 20–2, 31–26, 23–19, 14–18. *Drawn*

N When I showed the position at this stage to John T. Bradford, the veteran Internationalist, he suggested 7–10 to draw. Before I could appraise the move, Jules Leopold—a brilliant New York player, who was watching on, quickly floored it with this fancy flourish: 7–10, 26–22, 14–17! (Bradford's idea), 21–7*, 3–10, 20–16* (Leopold's idea, and very decisive!), 11–20, 22–17, down for the count. *White wins*

O 23–32, 26–23, 32–28 or 32–27, then 23–19. *White wins*

P 27–23 also wins, but I am featuring an alternative win to show a very instructive problem finish.

Q If 19–24, then 17–14, 24–31, 9–5, 18–9, 5–14, *White wins by First Position*. If 18–22, then 17–14, 22–17, 14–10, 17–22, 10–6, 22–18, 6–1, 19–24, 1–5. *White wins*

R A triple-barrelled finisher that clinches the win.

S Grover decides to take the long way home, still hoping for a win on the way in. Here, 31–27, 10–15 or 8–11, 27–23 draws at once.

GAME 22

9—14, 23—19, 14—18

BLACK: Kenneth Grover   WHITE: J. B. Hanson

BLACK		WHITE	
9—14	4—11	1—6 K	20—24 M
23—19	28—24	17—13	27—20
14—18	11—15 B,C	16—19	10—14
22—15	25—22 D	24—15	15—10
11—18	18—25	10—19	14—18
26—22	29—22	30—26 L	10—7
7—11	6—10 J	12—16	9—13
22—15	27—23	32—28	7—2
11—18	5—9	16—20	13—17
21—17	23—18	31—27	2—7
8—11 A	3—7	6—10	18—22 N
19—15	18—11	13—6	
10—19	7—16	2—9	
24—8	22—18	18—15	*Drawn*

Notes by WILLIAM F. RYAN

A Varies from the preceding game and is generally considered Black's best move.

B Undoubtedly best here, to thwart White from gaining a formidable center wedge. For example, if Black plays 3—7 here, then 24—19, and if 5—9, then 17—14, 9—13, 24—19, and in both instances Black loses all control of the center. At B, both 2—7 and 6—10 have been tried and found woefully weak.

At the 10th A.C.A. national tournament in 1939, at Flint, Mich., L. M. Lewis adopted 2—7 against Asa Long, and was soon in a bad game, viz: 2—7, 25—22, 18—25, 29—22, 5—9, 27—23, 7—10, 17—13, 9—14, 22—18, 14—17, 18—14, 17—22, 14—7, 3—10, 23—18, 12—16, 32—27, 16—20, 13—9, 6—13, 24—19, 13—17, 19—16, 10—15, 16—7, 15—19, 18—15, 19—24, 7—2, 24—28, 2—7, 28—32, 27—23, 32—27, 31—24, 20—27. *Drawn*—L. M. Lewis vs. Asa Long. Finely played.

C In his match with Newell W. Banks at Detroit in 1934, Asa Long tried 6—10, the game proceeding: 30—26, 10—15, 32—28, 2—7, 25—21, 1—6, 17—13, 7—10, and here Banks moved 26—23, Long drawing by 18—22 after much critical play. However, instead of Banks' 26—23, play instead 24—19, 15—24, 28—19, and Black's draw, if any, is very hard to find.

D Once again Hanson strikes out for uncharted seas, and this time he comes up with a four-masted windjammer. I can find no play on his 25—22 trade. The usual continuation is 30—26, on which I offer some new analysis of my own:

30—26	29—25 E	31—26	14—10	3—8
3—7	6—9*	22—31	31—26	2—6
17—14	24—20	32—28	8—11	11—7
6—10	9—13 F	31—24	26—22	9—13
25—21	25—21	28—3	10—7	*Drawn*
10—17	13—17* H	18—27	5—9	Wm. F. Ryan
21—14	26—23	3—8	7—3	
1—6	17—22*	27—31	22—18	

E 26—23, 18—22, 14—10, 7—14, 23—18, has been played to a draw by several prominent experts. The text is slightly stronger.

F 2—6, 25—21, 15—19* G, 32—28, 19—23*, 26—19, 18—22, also draws.

91

G 9–13 loses by 21–17*!, and 6–10 is soon frustrated by 26–23*, 10–17, 23–14*, 9–18, 21–14, 7–11 (18–22, 31–26), 31–26, 12–16, 27–24. *White wins*

H 2–6 now loses by 21–17, 13–22, 26–17, 6–10, 32–28*, 18–22, 27–24, 22–25, 31–27, 25–30, 27–23, 30–26, 23–19. *White wins*

J Certainly the best looking move, but it seems to get Black in a peck of trouble. The following seems to pan out better: 5–9, 27–23, 9–13, 17–14 (23–18, 3–7, 18–11, 7–16, 17–14, 16–19, 24–15, 6–10, 14–7, 2–25, 30–21, 1–6, 32–27, 6–10, etc., *Drawn*), 15–19, 24–15, 6–10, 15–6, 1–26, 31–22, 3–7, 23–19, 7–11 (7–10 draws too), 22–18, 11–16, 19–15, 13–17, 15–11, 17–22, 11–8, 16–19, 8–3, 12–16, 3–8, 22–26. *Drawn*

K 1–5, 24–20, 16–19, 17–13, 19–23, 13–6, 2–9, draws with careful play, but Grover did not like the looks of this continuation, and nobody can blame him! The move taken also draws —with a headache.

L 18–15, almost wins, but not quite: 18–15, 2–7, 32–27, 9–14, 30–25, 14–17*, 25–21, 17–22, 21–17, 7–10*, 15–11, 10–15*, 11–7, 6–10, 7–2, 15–18, 2–7, 10–15, 7–11, 22–25, 17–14, 25–30, 14–9, 19–23, 27–24, 23–27. *Drawn*

M A clever and necessary touch to sack the draw. Black is just in the nick of time to save the day.

N A remarkable crossboard game, flawlessly contested, in which Black has engineered a well earned escape. I don't believe that Mr. Grover was in a loss at any time in this game, although he had been skirting on thin ice ever since Hanson launched his innovation at D (25–22).

GAME 23

9–13, 22–18, 12–16

BLACK: Kenneth Grover WHITE: J. B. Hanson

9–13	21–14	17–22	8–3
22–18	7–10	15–11	23–14
12–16 A	14–7	22–26	15–10
18–14 B	3–10	23–19	14–7
10–17	18–15 G	16–23	3–10
21–14	9–14	18–15	21–25
8–12 C	15–6	26–31	10–15
23–18	2–9	27–18	25–30
16–20	22–18 H	13–17	15–19
24–19	13–17	11–8 J	30–26
11–16	31–27	4–11	32–27
27–23	17–21	15–8	26–31
6–9	26–22	17–22	19–23
25–21	9–13	18–15	31–24
1–6	18–9	22–26	28–19 K
29–25	5–14	30–23	
6–10	22–18	31–26	
25–22	14–17	23–18	*Drawn*
10–17	19–15	26–23	

Notes by WILLIAM F. RYAN

A Before the era of three-move restriction, this was more favored than 6–9 as a reply to 22–18. But no matter how you handle it, the Edinburgh Single is a sorely pressed debut for

Black. It is the Graveyard of Champions, and in this match, as in many others, it lives up to its reputation as the bogey game of draughts.

B While not a favored attack with the master minds of checkerdom, the text is much stronger than generally supposed. I beat Walter Hallman, the Hoosier grandmaster, with it in the 1938 Cedar Point (Ohio) Master's Tourney.

C This is a dead loss, and at best Black has only a feeble defense after it. Mr. Grover either forgot the right move here, or confused the opening moves with some other formational lead-off. These things happen in the best playing circles, particularly after a long layoff from serious play. Even the greatest of the great show remarkably poor form in their play every now and then, and this instance is merely a case of one of Grover's "Giddy" games. Despite the bad start, he managed to draw the game, which is something! The right move at *C* is:

16—19*	30—25 *E*	7—14	15—11	18—23
24—15	8—11	18—9	2—6	2—7
11—18	25—22	5—14	11—7	23—26
28—24	18—25	22—17	6—15	7—10
8—11	29—22	13—22	31—27	26—30
24—19	11—16	26—10	3—10	10—15
4—8	23—18	24—28 *F*	27—11	30—25
25—21	15—19	23—18	10—14	*Drawn*
11—15 *D*	27—23	16—19	11—7	Wm. F. Ryan
19—10	19—24	18—15	14—18	
6—15	14—10	19—23	7—2	

D I consider this much the best. The renowned Scotch master of the gay nineties, George Buchanan, once published play for a draw on 6—10, but I do not think well of it. It may be a loss.

94

E A powerful attack which I introduced against Walter Hallman in 1938. Published play shows a tame draw by 32—28. This is the one with the mustard on it.

F Here, Hallman went 16—20 and lost out by 23—18, 2—6, 18—15, 24—28, 21—17, 20—24, 17—13, 3—8, 31—26, 24—27, 32—23, 28—32, 10—7, 32—27, 23—19, 8—12, 26—22, 27—24, 7—3, 24—27, 3—7, 27—24, 22—17, 24—27, 7—11, 27—24, 17—14, 24—27, 14—9. *White wins.*

G Good enough, but the shortest win is: 30—25, 4—8 (2—7, 25—21, 7—11, 32—27, 4—8, 19—15, 10—19, 21—17, *White wins*), 25—21, 8—11, 32—27, 10—14, 22—17, 13—22, 26—10, 9—14, 18—9, 5—14, 10—6, 2—9, 19—15, 11—18, 21—17. *White wins*

H Hanson seems bent on making it hard for himself. Here, 31—27, 4—8, 19—15, 14—18, 23—14, 9—25, 30—21, 16—19, 15—10, is still an easy win.

J Going from bad to worse. With this move, Hanson allows his wily opponent to get a draw, but 15—10, 17—22, 10—7, still wins as Black cannot pitch 22—26 effectively.

K The problem in this game is to figure out how Hanson managed to pass by all the opportunities he had to press the win home. Grover must have had a rabbit's foot, a four-leaf clover, and a horseshoe tucked away in his britches to get out of such a predicament!

95

GAME 24

9—13, 22—18, 12—16

BLACK: J. B. Hanson   WHITE: Kenneth Grover

9—13	29—25	20—27	26—23
22—18	10—17	31—15	19—26
12—16	21—14	16—19 K	28—12
24—20 A	1—6	15—10	26—31
8—12	25—21	7—11	7—10
27—24	6—10	10—7	13—17 L
3—8	32—27	11—16	10—14
25—22 B	10—17	7—3	17—22
16—19 C	21—14	16—20	18—15
24—15	8—12 D	14—10	31—27
10—19	20—16 G	20—24	12—8
23—16	11—20	10—7	4—18
12—19	22—18	2—11	14—32
18—14	12—16 H, J	3—7	
6—10	27—24	11—16	White wins

Notes by WILLIAM F. RYAN

A Departs from the route of the previous game, and is the strongest of all White's attacks.

B Initiates a stubborn attack which is not easily shaken off. Mr. Grover was the first to discover its potent qualities, and published some fine play on it in "Let's Play Checkers." The

late A. J. Heffner shows this interesting draw on 18—14: 18—14, 10—17, 21—14, 6—10, 25—21, 10—17, 21—14, 1—6, 29—25, 6—10, 25—21, 10—17, 21—14, 16—19, 24—15, 11—27, 32—23, 2—6, 30—25, 6—9, 31—27, 9—18, 23—14, 13—17, 25—21, 8—11, 27—23, 11—15, 23—19, 15—24, 28—19, 7—11. *Drawn*

C Added notes are by Kenneth M. Grover.*

Jesse's 16—19 move is forced. The possible alternative 5—9 loses by 24—19, 11—15, 18—11, 8—24, 28—19, 7—11, 30—25, 10—15, 19—10, 6—15, 22—18, 15—22, 25—18, 2—6, 32—27. *White wins*

D 2—6 loses by 30—25, 6—9 E, 27—24, 9—18, 24—15, 5—9, 31—27, 9—14, 15—10, 14—17, 10—3, 17—21, 3—12, 21—30, 22—8. *White wins*

E 11—15, 25—21, 6—9, 14—10, 7—14, 22—17, 13—22, 26—10, 9—14 F, 10—7, 14—18, 31—26, 8—12, 20—16, 5—9, 7—2, 9—13, 2—7, 18—22, 26—17, 13—22, 16—11, 12—16, 7—10, 16—20, 10—7. *White wins*

F 19—24, 28—19, 15—24, 10—7, 24—28, 27—23, 28—32, 7—3, 8—12, 3—7, 32—28, 7—10, 28—24, 10—6, 9—13, 6—10, 24—28, 10—15, 28—24, 23—18. *White wins*

G Varies from Shearer's run for the draw by 27—23, 4—8, 23—16, 12—19, 26—23. The pitch 20—16 was the idea missed.

H In L.P.C. I offered 7—10, 14—7, 2—11, 27—24, 20—27, 31—8, 4—11, 18—14, 11—15, 14—10, 15—18, 10—7, 18—22, 26—17, 13—22, 7—2, 5—9, 2—6, 9—14, 6—10, 14—17, 10—15, 17—21, 28—24, 22—25, 24—19, 25—29. *Drawn*

J L.P.C. mentions that 2—6 will probably lose. After the game Jesse and I worked up the following draw: 2—6, 27—24, 20—27, 31—15, 7—11, 15—8, 4—11, 28—24, 13—17, 24—20, 6—9,

* Inasmuch as this game was a hi-lite of mine in "Let's Play Checkers," Willie suggested I take over. Most of the notes are lifted from *L.P.C.* —K.M.G.

14–10, 17–22, 26–17, 9–14, 18–9, 5–21, 10–7, 11–15 draws as Black has the move.

K Loses: 7–11 draws narrowly, but the draw at *H* is good enough.

L Up to here Jesse has followed the loss I have given in *L.P.C.* page 64, Note *M*.

GAME 25

9—14, 23—18, 14—23

BLACK: J. B. Hanson		WHITE: Kenneth Grover	
9—14	1—6	22—26	10—19
23—18 A	29—25	31—22	11—4
14—23	4—8	18—25	26—23
27—18	30—26	23—19	6—1
12—16 B	9—14	25—30 E	19—24
18—14 C	24—20	27—24	1—6
10—17	5—9	6—9	18—22
21—14	26—23	15—10	21—17
6—9	15—18	9—13	23—18
14—10 C	22—15	19—16	6—9
7—14	11—18	2—7	18—15
22—18 C	28—24 D	24—19	4—8
14—23	9—13	30—26	15—10
26—12	24—19	19—15	8—11
11—15	13—17	14—18	10—15
32—27	25—21	10—6	11—25
8—11	17—22	7—10	13—29
25—22	19—15	16—11	*Drawn*

Notes by JOHN B. STILES

A One of the so-called old "barred openings." This game is so weak for White that an inconsistent defense almost invariably results in capitulation.

B Considered by all as the strongest attack at Black's command.

C These moves are vitally necessary if the second player is to sustain a tenable formation.

D Looks like a weak one: 31—26 would be my choice here.

E Lets White off easy! 2—7, 27—24, 7—10, 20—16, 25—30, 16—11, 30—26, 11—4, 26—23. *Black wins*

GAME 26

9—14, 23—18, 14—23

BLACK: Kenneth Grover		WHITE: J. B. Hanson	
9—14	22—18	4—8	22—18
23—18	14—23	30—26	13—17
14—23	26—12	5—9 C	18—9
27—18	11—15	26—23	5—14
12—16 A	25—22 B	1—5	25—22
18—14	9—14	32—27	17—26
10—17	29—25	9—13	31—22
21—14	8—11	27—24	14—17
6—9	24—19	11—16	22—13
14—10	15—24	24—20	2—6
7—14	28—19	8—11	19—15 D
			Drawn

Notes by JOHN B. STILES

A 5—9 is another good move that can be made at this point.

B Safer, in my judgment, than 32—27 as played in game 25.

C Interesting and apparently a safe deviation from the text books.

D A well played game on the part of both players in an opening that is always troublesome.

GAME 27

11—16, 21—17, 16—20

BLACK: Kenneth Grover   WHITE: J. B. Hanson

11—16	28—19	2—9	28—19
21—17	4—8	26—23	11—15
16—20 A	22—18	9—13	16—11
17—13	14—17	31—26 C	15—31
8—11	29—25	1—6	11—2
22—18	8—11	32—28	10—15
9—14	19—16	10—15	23—18
18—9	12—19	18—14	15—19
5—14	23—16	6—10	18—14
25—22	17—21	14—9	13—17
11—15	25—22	15—19	22—13
24—19 B	6—9	9—6	31—22
15—24	13—6	19—24 D	Drawn

Notes by John B. Stiles

A Leads to a fairly even game but was rarely adopted prior to the inception of the three-move style of play.

B Here is an interesting variation: 29—25, 7—11, 25—21, 4—8, 30—25, 11—16, 24—19, 15—24, 28—19, 3—7, 19—15, 10—19, 22—18, 6—9, 13—6, 2—9, 32—28, 8—11, 25—22, 7—10, 27—24. *Drawn*—Newell W. Banks *vs.* John B. Stiles.

C 23–19 confines Black to a narrow groove via: 10–15, 19–10, 7–23, 16–7, 3–10, 27–18, 1–5, 31–27, 5–9, 27–24, 20–27, 32–23, 10–14, 18–15. *Drawn*–J. B. Hanson.

D If 11–15, then 16–11!, 7–16, 6–2, 10–14, 2–6, 3–8, 22–17, 13–31, 6–9, 31–24, 9–4, 19–26, 28–12. *Drawn*–John B. Stiles.

GAME 28

11—16, 21—17, 16—20

BLACK: J. B. Hanson		WHITE: Kenneth Grover	
11—16	4—8	5—14	11—16
21—17	18—9	13—9	19—15
16—20	5—14	15—18	10—19
17—14 A	25—22	26—22	17—10
10—17 B	8—11	18—27	19—23
22—13	13—9	32—23	6—2
9—14	11—15	10—15	18—22
25—22	19—16	16—12	2—6
8—11	12—19	7—10	16—20
29—25	23—16	25—21	10—7
11—15	1—5	2—7	3—10
24—19	27—23 D	22—17	6—15
15—24	20—24	7—11	27—24
28—19	30—25	9—6	20—27
6—10	14—17	15—18	
22—18	22—13	23—19	Drawn

Notes by JOHN B. STILES

A Whether this, or 17—13, as adopted in previous game, is best is a matter of conjecture. The experts themselves are partial to both.

B 9–18, 23–14, 10–17, 22–13, 8–11, 24–19, 7–10, 25–22, 11–15, 26–23, 15–24, 28–19, 4–8, 22–18, 10–14, 18–9, 5–14, 29–25, 8–11, 25–22, 14–17, 31–26 *C*, 11–16, 22–18, 2–7, 18–14, 7–10, 14–7, 3–10, 23–18, 16–23, 26–19, 17–22, 18–15, 22–26, 30–23, 12–16, etc. *Drawn*–John B. Stiles.

C Improves 22–18, 17–22, 18–15, 11–18, 23–14 and now E. Wylie played 1–5 in his match with Willie Ryan and lost. Instead he missed a problem win by 3–7, 14–9, 7–10, 32–28, 10–14, 19–15, 14–17, etc.

D A plausible continuation might be: 27–24, 20–27, 32–23, 14–17, 22–13, 5–14, 13–9, 15–19, 31–27, 14–18, etc. *Drawn* –John B. Stiles.

105

GAME 29

9—13, 23—19, 10—14

BLACK: J. B. Hanson		WHITE: Kenneth Grover	
9—13	19—16	2—7	31—24
23—19	12—19	30—26	15—18
10—14 A	24—8	11—15	21—17
27—23	4—11	22—18	14—21
11—16	23—19 D	15—22	23—14
22—17 B	6—10	26—17	21—25
13—22	25—22	10—15	24—19
25—9	11—15	17—10	25—30
5—14	26—23	7—14	19—15
29—25 C	15—24	16—11	30—26
16—20	28—19	1—6	14—10
32—27	7—11	27—24	6—9 E
8—11	19—16	20—27	*Drawn*

Notes by JOHN B. STILES

A A comparatively easy game, slightly in favor of the second player.

B The text is correct. If 24—20, 6—9, 20—11, 8—24, 28—19, 14—17 and Black is best.

C If 24—20, then 6—10, 20—11, 8—24, etc. is the proper continuation.

D 25—22 is the line most generally adopted at this point and would run into game 10, colors reversed.

E Thus ended a match contested by two of the World's foremost exponents of the highly scientific game of Checkers. Mr. Grover becomes the new Pacific Coast Champion after a long and honorable reign by the great veteran, Jesse B. Hanson.

The Match

HAVING engaged such stars as Willie Ryan, Alex Cameron, Harold Freyer, Newell W. Banks and numerous others at one time or another in my career, it was a pleasant relief to sit back and watch two such masters as Grover and Hanson perform. Although I know both players very well, I learned much about each by observing them closely in this great encounter. For the benefit of the reader, I have set down some of my conclusions and opinions regarding the match and the two principals. It is always interesting to see a crossboard or "natural" player parry moves with a so-called "book" player. I say so-called because all master players are, and have to be, "book" players. However, the amount of book play one master may know is often so great in comparison to his contemporaries that he is at once tagged a "book" player. I believe all will agree that in this match Mr. Grover represented the crossboard type of player and Mr. Hanson the man with more knowledge of published play, especially on the two-move games. Personally, I have always held that no player alive today excels Grover as a natural crossboard performer, and it is hard to name a player with more knowledge of go-as-you-please and two-move play than Hanson. Hence, at least as far as I was concerned, this match was the long-awaited showdown between the natural player and the man with the knowledge. This may be over-simplifying the matter a bit, but I believe that in its broader aspects such was the case. There might be some who will say that since this was a match on three-move restriction, Grover, as the crossboard player, would have the edge, and with them I would be inclined to agree.

Since we still know so little of three-move checkers, it is largely a matter of crossboard play, rather than memory and knowledge—and this, I think, is all to the good. I believe the Grover-Hanson type of match (or any three-move match) will be found far more interesting and instructive than a Wyllie-Martins affairs or a Pomeroy-Jordan contest. Three-move is progress and progress is necessary if any sport or pastime is to meet with popular approval and truly flourish.

As I watched young Grover matching wits with the veteran Hanson, I also seemed to see a splendid representative of the modern school of players struggling with a valiant warrior of the old guard. Grover belongs to that hardy band of youngsters who have been educated in tough three-movers. They include Ryan, Hallman, Freyer, Case, Rubin, Hunt, et al. Jesse carried the banner for an older group who had gained their fame in other years at two-move and go-as-you-please. Though many of these masters are gone to their reward, such stalwarts as Banks, Bradford, Long (a young veteran), Ginsberg, O'Grady and some others are still with us. So, to me, this was the old school versus the new as well as the crossboard player against the man of knowledge.

Some of my readers may enjoy a description of these two greats at the board. Mr. Hanson has the ideal temperament for match checkers. He sits at the board perfectly calm and cool and always seems in perfect command of the situation. No matter what his position on the board may be, he never gets ruffled or nervous. Indeed, Jesse appears exactly like a sphinx at the board. When he finally decides to move, he is deliberate and positive in his manner and one gets the impression that without a shadow of doubt the best move has been made. Kenneth, on the other hand, is inclined at times to be just a shade nervous and his thoughts seem to be conveyed to the

109

spectator—but this is merely an illusion. I believe it is only natural for the "book" player to be more calm as he usually knows where he is, while the crossboard player must do more thinking and analyzing, and consequently tends to show his thoughts more by his expressions and mannerisms. Although Grover emerged the winner, it was by a comparatively close margin, and Mr. Hanson proved he is still to be reckoned with, and, because of his fine performance, arose from the table with the cheers of the spectators ringing in his ears.

I believe that because of this victory Grover is now in a position where he cannot be ignored in future discussions of the world championship situation. Although it is quite possible that I am prejudiced, I believe that he is the equal of any player in the world at the three-move restriction style of play, and that he is superior to any player across the board at any style. There you have a short description of these two great masters. Of course, there will be those who will differ with me in many of my conclusions, but it is this difference of opinion which makes matches and tourneys both possible and interesting.

T. W.

The Committee of 100

WE wish to take this opportunity to thank the following loyal supporters of the game, whose efforts and generosity made this event the great success it was.

ALEX McKAY · PARKS HERZOG · AL FLOWERS · LOUIS BURT · ARTHUR R. JOHNSON · C. O. PATRICK · SHERIFF LEE CROFT · RANSOM MINKLER (PRES. CHAM. OF COMMERCE, ABERDEEN, WASHINGTON) · FRANK W. AZEVEDO · HARRY S. FASNACHT · MR. AND MRS. FLOYD PAYNE · ARNOLD GALLUB · A. PASHOS · T. R. JONES · ALBERT GERMAIN · B. A. BONNER · REX B. WOOD · WILLIAM FOSTNAUGHT · F. R. BENE · ROBERT NELSON · CHARLES I. PACE · R. MUNZINGER · DR. LEWIS F. SCHREIBER · MEL C. BLACKBURN · WILLIAM IRWIN · P. H. THOMPSON · J. F. WRIGHT · THOMAS QUINLAN · B. T. CLIFTON · JAMES C. BROWN · JOHN DAZIO · A. J. GIANCOLA · JUDD L. PALMER · H. M. GRINE · CHARLES J. SIMON · H. N. McKENZIE · ROBERT MARTIN · DR. W. L. NEWTON · CHARLES C. INKE · TACOMA CHECKER CLUB (CROFT HOTEL) · FRED REWOLDT · E. L. RICE · IRVING DAVIDS · MERWIN WRIDE · DR. EDWARD PHILLIPS · CHARLES B. WINTER · JAMES J. LAVERY · EDWARD T. FRANKEL · EMIN ELAM · WILLIE RYAN · JOHN B. STILES · MARGRET LYDA · THE SEATTLE C & C CLUB · DAVID THOMSON · FERRY FLODSEN · MILES R. SMITH · ANGUS DAVISON · ANDREW DEBY · JOHN ISAAC-

SON · JOSEPH VIERA · CLIFFORD E. WOODARD ·
E. A. BRUHN · BEN BOLAND · J. A. HAMMOND ·
N. E. BOWIN · WILLIAM WESSON · GENE MASIE ·
IVAN COE · JOHNNIE MITCHELL · JOHN A. OLSON ·
E. ERICKSON · I. MISHER · HENRY CONOVER ·
R. WHITNEY · A. ZULIN · H. DALEY · GEORGE GRAN-
GER · JOE MURPHY · D. JEFFERY · WILLIAM COURT-
NEY · CHARLES OAKLEY · C. M. HINOTE · BILL
FITZHENRY · A. J. BANKS · GEORGE L. GORDON ·
FAUSTO DALUMI · B. E. GARRETSON · HARRY LIEBER-
MAN · AL HODES · L. N. LYDICK · H. B. BROOKS ·
GEORGE S. CALLIS · MAURICE SEAVEY · M. MENEL ·
T. A. KNUTSON · GEORGE M. GIBSON · (MRS.) F. J.
HOSPIDOR · JAMES A. BUSH · THOMAS ALBERT ·
CLARENCE L. STONE

TWENTIETH CENTURY OPENINGS

Edited by

KENNETH M. GROVER

THE importance of the opening moves cannot be over-estimated in the study of scientific Checkers. In the following pages the reader will find a working introduction to each of the 137 three-move openings.

Few players will have the time to make a thorough study of all the complete games at hand which make up the modern three-move restriction but a knowledge of the initial moves will suffice to set one on the right road—and that is what counts.

Many of the openings transpose into one another and this point will act as an additional time saver and work eliminator. I have given numerous examples of transpositions but there are countless others that I feel sure the reader will soon discover.

(1) 9—13, 21—17, 5—9

9—13	29—25 B
21—17	9—14 C
5—9 A	23—18
25—21	14—23
11—15	27—11

A Favors Black but not hard to handle. Black cramps the man on 17. See opening (85) at B.

B 23—18, 1—5, (if 12—16, 18—11, 8—15, go 24—20) 18—11, 8—15, 24—19.

C 15—19, 24—15, 10—19, 23—16, 12—19, 17—14.

○

(2) 9—13, 21—17, 6—9

9—13	30—25
21—17	9—14
6—9 A	24—19
25—21	15—24
11—15	28—19

A It should be noted Black, the stronger side, can force this opening and the above as an offshoot from the 11—15, 21—17, 9—13, opening after White answers 25—21. These openings are commonly called the Switcher and requires careful study by the White side. See opening (85) at B.

○

(3) 9—13, 22—17, 13—22

9—13	18—11
22—17	8—15
13—22 A	21—17 B
25—18	4—8
11—15	23—19 C

A This opening is considered equal with chances to vary for both sides at many points throughout the game.

B Another move would be 29—25, 4—8, 25—22, 5—9, 23—18, 8—11, to a draw.

C Choice would be 17—13 or 24—20.

114

(4) 9—13, 22—18, 6—9

9—13	30—25
22—18	11—15
6—9 A	8—11
26—22 B	8—15
1—6	22—17 C

A The first two moves form the Edinburgh and any opening formed by it has "super duper" strength for White. All the 9—13, 22—18 starters are classed in the weakest contingent for Black.

B Another powerful alternative for White would be 18—14, 10—17, 21—14, 9—18, 23—14, 12—16, 26—22, (if 24—20, 1—6, 25—22, 6—9) 11—15, 24—20, 7—11, and 30—26, or 28—24, or 27—24, must be handled very carefully by the Black pieces. Opening is same as 9—13, 23—18, 6—9, 26—23. See (9).

C Continuing 13—22, 25—11, 7—16, 29—25, and now 4—8 must be played to draw. Play is given in "Let's Play Checkers" on winning against 9—14, or 10—14.

○

(5) 9—13, 22—18, 10—15

9—13	24—20 B
22—18	5—9
10—15 A	28—24
25—22	10—14
6—10	22—17 C

A Ginsberg's suggestion for studying checkers was to be sure of the real weak openings and sometimes took chances of not knowing all the play on those classified even.

B Watch for 23—19, forcing 11—16, 18—11, 16—23, 27—18, and now be sure to jump 8—15, 18—11, and 7—16.

C See 9—13, 24—20, 5—9, and 9—13, 24—20, 10—14. See (21 and 23).

115

(6) 9—13, 22—18, 11—15

9—13	21—17 B
22—18	13—22
11—15 A	25—11
18—11	7—16
8—15	24—20 C, D, E

A White has a powerful debut with many choices of offensive attacks.

B If 24—20, 7—11, 25—22, 5—9 shown in Ryan's Modern Encyclopedia.

C A strong departure from usual play is 24—19 which can be met by 4—8.

D A powerhouse is 29—25 which is met by 5—9. From here I suggest you study Ryan's fine play as this game is plenty "tuff" for Black.

E And now be sure to move 3—8.

○

(7) 9—13, 22—18, 12—16

9—13	27—24
22—18	3—8
12—16 A	25—22 C
24—20 B	16—19
8—12	23—16

A Of all the 9—13, 22—18 openings this is considered best for Black. Next in line I would rank 9—13, 22—18, 10—15, then it would be a choice between 9—13, 22—18, 6—9, and 9—13, 22—18, 11—15. I believe the latter is the weakest of the Edinburghs.

B A tricky line is 18—14, 10—17, 21—14 and now 16—19 must be made. And at B if 25—22 is made move 16—19, or at B if 24—19, 8—12. See (20).

C If 24—19, 11—15 or if 18—14 at C move 10—17, 21—14, 6—10, 25—21, 10—17, 21—14, 1—6, 29—25, 16—19.

(8) 9—13, 23—18, 5—9

9—13	30—26
23—18	11—16
5—9 A	24—19
26—23 B	8—11
10—14	28—24

A Practically puts the game on an even keel with White having more room for varying.

B If 27—23, 10—14.

O

(9) 9—13, 23—18, 6—9

9—13	30—26
23—18	11—15
6—9 A	18—11
26—23 B	8—15
1—6	22—17

A White has a dreadnought.

B Now the same as 9—13, 22—18, 6—9, 26—22. At Note B 18—15 would be the same as 9—13, 23—19, 6—9, 19—15. Continue: 10—19, 24—15, 11—18, 22—15, 7—11, 26—22, 11—18, 22—15, 3—7, 25—22, 1—6, 28—24, 8—11 and is a line shown to me by Willie Ryan. Trunk has the power. See (4 and 14).

O

(10) 9—13, 23—18, 10—15

9—13	32—27
23—18	5—9 B
10—15 A	18—14
27—23	9—18
6—10	23—14

A White emerges very strong.

B Secondary choice used by Hanson and myself is 1—6, 18—14, 10—17, 21—14, 15—18, 22—15, 11—18, 26—22, 12—16.

117

(11) 9—13, 23—18, 11—15

9—13	22—17
23—18	13—22
11—15A	25—11
18—11	7—16
8—15	29—25B

A Favoring White but not as strong as one might believe on first appearance. There is a similarity to the 6—9 line of 9—13, 22—18 that White can force but real power for White is only an illusion.

B Or continue 21—17, 4—8, 17—13, 16—20.

O

(12) 9—13, 23—18, 12—16

9—13	21—14
23—18	6—10
12—16A	24—20B
18—14	10—17
10—17	25—21C

A White has the pull and makes the variations.

B Many prefer 27—23, 10—17, 24—19, 8—12, 25—21, 1—6, 21—14, 13—17, 22—13, 6—9, 13—6, 2—27, 32—23, and 7—10.

C Continue 1—6, 21—14, 6—9.

O

(13) 9—13, 23—19, 5—9

9—13	18—11
23—19	8—15
5—9A	25—22
22—18B	9—14
11—15	27—23

A An even game which can easily be transposed into other openings.

B 27—23, 11—15, 22—18, 15—22, 25—18, 8—11, 19—15, 10—19, 24—8, 4—11, 32—27, 6—10, 18—14.

118

(14) 9—13, 23—19, 6—9

9—13	22—18
23—19	11—15
6—9 A	18—9 C
27—23 B	5—14
9—14	25—22 D

A An advantage for White but the early exchanges simplify matters for Black.

B Just as good would be 19—15 (see 9—13, 23—18, 6—9). See (9).

C 18—11, 8—15, 23—18, 15—22.

D Now 7—11, 30—25, 1—5, 22—17, (if 32—27, 11—16).

(15) 9—13, 23—19, 10—14

9—13	22—17
23—19	13—22
10—14 A	25—9
27—23	5—14
11—16	29—25 B

A White has a very slight edge mostly in control of choice of lines but so many swaps in the early part of the game make matters easy for Black. Really an open game. Easily transposed to other openings.

B Or 24—20.

(16) 9—13, 23—19, 11—16

9—13	30—26
23—19	8—11
11—16 A	19—16
26—23 B	12—19
16—20	24—8

A Considered equal but I prefer handling the White forces.

B Of the same magnitude would be 27—23, 16—20, 32—27, 8—11, 19—16, 12—19, 24—8, 4—11, 23—18, (if 23—19, 6—9) 10—15, 18—14, 6—9, 22—18.

119

(17) 9—13, 24—19, 5—9

9—13	22—18
24—19	15—22
5—9 A	25—18
28—24	1—5
11—15	29—25 B

A Black has an uphill fight but White must limit its scope to keep a good advantage.

B Fine play by Edwin Hunt continues: 8—11, 24—20, (if 25—22, 11—16, 24—20, 3—8, 20—11, 8—24, 27—20) 3—8, 19—16, 12—19, 23—16, 8—12, 27—23, 12—19, 23—16, 10—14, 26—23, 6—10, 25—22, (16—12, 13—17) 14—17, to a draw.

○

(18) 9—13, 24—19, 6—9

9—13	18—11
24—19	8—24
6—9 A	28—19
22—18 B	4—8
11—15	25—22

A White can decide what avenue his opponent is to travel and also has a slight pull.

B If 28—24, 11—15 we have another opening: 9—13, 24—19, 11—15, 28—24, same (19).

(19) 9—13, 24—19, 11—15

9—13	22—18 *B*
24—19	15—22
11—15 *A*	25—18
28—24 *B*	9—14
6—9 *C*	18—9

A The ramifications of this opening are many and are worthwhile looking into for knowledge and a pleasant sojourn.

B Not as satisfactory is 22—18, 15—22, 25—18, 8—11, and now 26—22 or 28—24 runs into a Single Corner opening favoring Black slightly: 11—15, 22—18, 15—22, 25—18, 8—11, 24—19, 9—13 and now 26—22 or 28—24.

C Not 8—11 as White puts terrific pressure by 23—18. See (18).

D Equal choice among the experts is the 23—18 move. Now 1—6, 18—11, 7—23, 26—19 (or 27—18, 12—16) 8—11, 32—28, 11—16, 19—15, 10—19, 24—15, 3—7, 30—26 and 7—11.

O

(20) 9—13, 24—19, 11—16

9—13	18—14
24—19	10—17
11—16 *A*	21—14
22—18	6—9 *C*
8—11 *B*	26—22

A Leads to a strong development for White.

B Now the same as 9—13, 22—18, 12—16, 24—19, 8—12. See (7).

C A key idea to loosen the foothold.

121

(21) 9—13, 24—20, 5—9

9—13	25—22
24—20	6—10 B
5—9 A	27—24 C
22—18	10—14
10—15	22—17

A Black must carefully defend his game.

B Now into a 9—13, 22—18, 10—15 opening by 25—22, 6—10, 24—20, 5—9. Also see 9—13, 24—20, 10—14. See (5 and 23).

C 28—24 is also very strong by 10—14, 22—17, 13—22, 26—10, 7—14, 30—26, 15—22, 26—10, 2—7 and 29—25 or 10—6 are both strong for White.

◯

(22) 9—13, 24—20, 6—9

9—13	23—18
24—20	8—11
6—9 A	27—23
28—24 B	1—6
11—15	32—28 C

A White is strong and has plenty of chances to play original lines to good success.

B E. F. Hunt adopted this move against Asa Long in a championship match.

C Continue 3—8, 23—19, 9—14, 18—9, 5—14, 22—17.

◯

(23) 9—13, 24—20, 10—14

9—13	22—17
24—20	13—22
10—14 A	25—9
28—24 B	5—14
6—10 C	29—25

A This interesting three mover is strong for White and offers plenty of action.

B To vary go 22—18, 5—9, 25—22, 6—10, 28—24, 10—15, 22—17 and we are in a position arising from several openings, for example: 9—13, 22—18, 10—15 and 9—13, 24—20, 5—9. See (5 and 21).

C In the first National Checker Association tourney I drew with 7—10 but I believe our trunk is more solid although 7—10 is accepted as a good draw.

(24) 9—13, 24—20, 10—15

9—13	21—17
24—20	16—19
10—15 *A*	17—14 *C*
23—18 *B*	6—9
12—16	27—24

A Black is slightly inferior.

B 28—24, 6—10, 23—19, 5—9, 26—23, 1—5, 21—17, 9—14, 25—21, 5—9, 32—28.

C Now into a 10—15, 23—18, 12—16 game by 21—17, 16—19, 17—14, 9—13, 24—20. See (77)

○

(25) 9—13, 24—20, 11—15

9—13	25—11
24—20	8—15
11—15 *A*	21—17 *B*
22—17	5—9
13—22	17—13 *C*

A Puts the game on an even keel and an easy game to manipulate with either side.

B Option here is 29—25, 4—8, 25—22, 8—11, to a draw.

C Group this game with the 11—15, 22—17, 9—13 opening if 24—20 is made. See (89).

○

(26) 9—14, 22—17, 5—9

9—14	25—22
22—17	14—17
5—9 *A*	21—14
17—13	9—25
1—5 *B*	29—22 *C*

A Favoring White with many opportunities to drift into other three movers.

B Now the same as 9—14, 22—17, 6—9, 17—13 (24—19 usual choice) 1—6 (27).

C Continue: 10—15, 23—18, (22—17 is also good) 11—16, 18—11, 8—15 is a familiar landing via 11—15, 22—17, 15—19, 23—16, 12—19, 24—15, 10—19, 25—22, 8—11, 27—23, 4—8, 23—16, 11—20, 22—18, 8—11, 32—27. We have the same position but with colors reversed and is a Dyke game. See (91).

(27) 9—14, 22—17, 6—9

9—14	28—24
22—17	13—22
6—9 A	25—9
24—19 B	5—14
9—13	29—25

A Black must earn his draw unless he knows some published play on this opening.

B White can force the above opening by going 17—13, then 1—6, same. (26) Text is same as 10—14, 24—19, 6—10, 22—17. (53)

○

(28) 9—14, 22—17, 11—15

9—14	24—15
22—17	10—19
11—15 A	23—16
25—22 B	12—19
15—19	17—10 C

A Even, but Black may have more selections to choose from. Along many lines both sides have variety.

B 23—19 runs into an honest to goodness "go as you please" game. (88, 100, 98)

C See openings 29, 91.

○

(29) 9—14, 22—17, 11—16

9—14	25—22
22—17	11—15
11—16 A	17—13
24—19 B	15—24
8—11	28—19 C

A Called the Pioneer giving White diversity on many variations plus a slight pull. Both opponents have equal chances for victory as the wins on this game are on a par. This is a very important opening to study as the games that possibly arise from it come from over one third of all the three move opening. On many lines Black takes control and chooses the path White must take. See "Let's Play Checkers" at Mid-Game Structure, page 92.

B Some players prefer 25—22 and Black
can swap 15—19 or move 8—11.

C See openings (84, 86, 108, 111, 119).

O

(30) 9—14, 22—18, 5—9

9—14	24—19
22—18	8—11
5—9 A	28—24 C
25—22 B	16—20
11—16	22—17

A An even game and when playing Black in my exhibitions essay it often.

B For simplicity try 24—19, 11—15, to an even game. (38, 41)

C If White desires to release the pressure in the single corner, the continuity is 22—17, 9—13, 18—9 13—22, 26—17, 6—22, 30—26, 11—15, 26—17, 15—24, 28—19, 10—14, 17—10, 7—14, 29—25, 4—8, 25—22, 8—11, 31—26, 2—6, 22—18, 11—15, 18—11, 14—18 to an easy finish.

O

(31) 9—14, 22—18, 10—15

9—14	26—22 B
22—18	15—18
10—15 A	22—15
18—9	11—18
5—14	21—17 C

A Strong for White. Black must overdevelop his double corner causing a weakness at this section.

B The stinger. Same as 10—15, 23—18, 9—14, 18—9, 5—14, 26—23. (75)

C White can keep the game cloistered by going 31—26 but 21—17 is the favored.

125

(32) 9—14, 22—18, 11—15

9—14	25—22
22—18	8—11
11—15A	22—17
18—9B	11—16
5—14	24—20C

A Can be classified as an even position.

B The other jump 18—11 is also taken.

C And now 3—8 is the move. White could have varied and taken 17—13 instead of 24—20.

○

(33) 9—14, 22—18, 11—16

9—14	24—19B
22—18	8—11
11—16A	25—22
18—9	11—15
5—14	29—25C

A White can launch a few powerful attacks but knowing these Black should be able to wiggle through.

B We arrive at 9—14, 24—19, 11—16, 22—18, 8—11, 18—9, 5—14, at the next move. (40) In lieu of 24—19, a good preference is 25—22, 16—19, 24—15, 10—19, 23—16, 12—19, 22—17, 6—10, 27—24, 2—6, 24—15, 10—19, 17—10, 7—14. (115)

C Now 15—24, 28—19, 4—8, 22—18, 8—11.

○

(34) 9—14, 23—18, 14—23

9—14	18—14
23—18	10—17
14—23A	21—14
27—18	6—9
12—16B	14—10C

A White in jumping dislodges a very important apex piece (on 27), leaving a weak formation.

B Strong also but not usually made is 5—9, 24—20.

C White must play very carefully from here.

126

(35) 9—14, 23—19, 5—9

9—14	22—18
23—19	15—22
5—9 A	25—18
27—23 B	7—11
11—15 C	26—22

A Black has the choice for the mid-game.

B 22—17 is the Fife from 11—15, 23—19, if Black so decides: continue 9—14, 22—17 and 5—9.

C Into the Defiance—the 5—9 line. A "go as you please game" from 11—15, 23—19, 9—14, 27—23, 5—9. See (38, 100).

O

(36) 9—14, 23—19, 11—16

9—14	30—26
23—19	8—11
11—16 A	19—16
26—23	12—19
16—20 B, C	24—8

A Most variations lead to equal positions.

B Popular is 5—9, 22—18, 16—20, 25—22, 7—11.

C 6—9 is the same as 10—14, 23—19, 11—16, 26—23, 6—10. See (51).

O

(37) 9—14, 23—19, 14—18

9—14	26—22
23—19	7—11
14—18 A	22—15
22—15	11—18
11—18	21—17 B

A Black plays defensively but not a real hard three mover.

B Now 8—11, 19—15.

(38) 9—14, 24—19, 5—9

9—14	18—11
24—19	8—24
5—9 A	28—19
22—18 B	4—8
11—15	25—22

A An even game which can easily run in the Double Corner line of 9—14, 22—18, 5—9, 24—19. See (30).

B 27—24, 11—15 is the 5—9 line of Defiance. See (35, 100).

○

(39) 9—14, 24—19, 11—15

9—14	18—9
24—19	5—14
11—15 A	28—19
22—18	8—11 B
15—24	25—22

A Black has the attack and secures a strong mid-game.

B Arriving at a Second Double Corner position, e.g. 11—15, 24—19, 15—24, 28—19, 8—11, 22—18, 9—14, 18—9, 5—14. See (101).

○

(40) 9—14, 24—19, 11—16

9—14	18—9
24—19	5—14 C
11—16 A	25—22
22—18	11—15
8—11 B	29—25

A Gives White the pull.

B More complicated but popular with many is 5—9, 26—22, 7—11, 22—17, 16—20, 17—13, 11—15.

C Now transposed into the following game: 9—14, 22—18, 11—16, 18—9, 5—14, 24—19, 8—11. See (33).

○

(41) 9—14, 24—20, 5—9

9—14	28—24
24—20	15—22
5—9 A	26—10
22—18 B	7—14
10—15 C	25—22

A An equal game.

B White can force this from 9—14, 22—18, 5—9, 24—20. See (30).

C More often chosen is 11—16, 20—11, 8—22, 25—18, 4—8, 28—24, 8—11, 29—25, 10—15.

(42) 9—14, 24—20, 10—15

9—14	25—9
24—20	5—14
10—15 A	29—25
22—18 B	7—10 C
15—22	25—22 D

A My comments on this opening in the N.C.A. Tourney Book were "The White Side controls the attacks on this opening, none of which reflects any paralyzing assaults on the Black defenses." Inadvertently the book gave credit to my associate Tommy Wiswell for my notes and play.

B Optional is 22—17, 7—10, 25—22, 3—7.

C This opening can now be studied with 9—14, 24—20, 11—15, 22—18, 15—22, 25—9, 5—14, 29—25, 7—11. (43)

D It might do well to remember a few more moves in this opening: 6—9, 27—24, 3—7, 24—19, 11—16.

(43) 9—14, 24—20, 11—15

9—14	25—9
24—20	5—14
11—15 A	29—25
22—18	7—11 B
15—22	25—22

A Black on defensive.

B Same as 9—14, 24—20, 10—15 opening. (42)

(44) 9—14, 24—20, 11—16

9—14	22—18 B
24—20	15—22
11—16 A	25—9
20—11	5—14
8—15	29—25

A Not a hard three mover for Black but he must play defensively.

B Some prefer 23—18, another good line with opportunities for crossboard play.

(45) 10—14, 22—17, 7—10

10—14	24—20 B,C
22—17	14—18
7—10 A	23—14
17—13	9—18
3—7	26—23

A Good for White but the seasoned players know the dope on this opening.

B 25—22, 14—17, 21—14, 9—25, 29—22, 10—15, 23—18, 6—10.

C 24—19, 11—16, 25—22, 14—17.

○

(46) 10—14, 22—17, 14—18

10—14	17—13 B
22—17	5—9
14—18 A	21—17
23—14	11—15
9—18	25—21 C

A The experts are ironing out the kinks in this three mover which is strong for White. White has a multitude of attacks.

B If 26—23, 6—9, 23—14, 9—18, 30—26, 5—9, 17—14, 9—13, 26—23, 1—5. If at B, 24—19, 11—16. See (55).

C 26—22, 12—16, 17—14, 1—5, 22—17, 8—11, 25—21, 18—23, 27—18, 15—22, 14—10, 6—15, 13—6, 2—9, 17—13, 9—14, 13—9, 4—8 and we have play that was first offered by the late Vince Connolly, and William Link who wows them down in New York. My associate, Mr. Wiswell, showed much beautiful play on this line and was the first player to publish the right continuation.

(47) 10—14, 22—18, 6—10

10—14	24—20 B
22—18	16—19 C
6—10 A	23—16
25—22	14—23
12—16	26—19 D

A This opening is powerful for White. I believe the champions have plenty of "cooks" in store for Black and Time will bring them out.

B Strong preference is given for this line but 22—17 leads to new developments and is good also. The text runs into published play to a game called "The White Doctor." See Note D.

C Black goes a piece down to avoid a terrific cramp on the single corner side.

D 8—12, 22—17 (if 31—26, 11—15, 27—23, 15—24, 28—19, 4—8, 29—25, 8—11, 23—18, and now 9—14) 9—14. The key to remember is going 9—14 early on one variation and holding back on another.

Published play runs into these games via: 11—16, 22—18, 10—14, 25—22, 8—11, 24—20, 16—19, 23—16, 14—23, 26—19, 6—10, etc. See (49).

○

(48) 10—14, 22—18, 11—15

10—14	26—22 B, C
22—18	6—10
11—15 A	22—17
18—11	1—6
8—15	23—19

A White has a slight advantage but must not overstep the initiative as Black also has winning chances.

B 24—20, 6—10, 28—24, 1—6, 23—19, 9—13, 25—22 (if 26—22, 15—18, 22—15, 12—16, should win for Black—Kear's Encyclopedia) 6—9, 29—25, 4—8, 26—23, now 14—17 or 14—18.

C Same as 11—15, 23—18, 10—14, 18—11, 8—15, 26—23. (95)

(49) 10—14, 22—18, 11—16

10—14	24—19
22—18	8—11
11—16ᴬ	19—15
25—22	4—8
16—20ᴮ	22—17ᶜ

A White is best and has a wide choice of lines to play. He can vary at many stages. Black beware.

B 8—11, 24—20 is the White Doctor again, but is best to be avoided. (47)

C Continue 22—17, 9—13, 17—10, 7—14, 18—9, 5—14, 29—25, 11—18, 26—22, 2—7, 22—15, 7—10.

O

(50) 10—14, 23—18, 14—23

10—14	32—27
23—18	16—20ᴮ
14—23ᴬ	26—23
27—18	6—10
12—16	30—26

A Weak for White because of a loose formation after losing an apex piece on 27. Considered better for White than the similar 9—14, 23—18, 14—23 opening.

B 9—14, 18—9, 5—14, 26—23, 16—20, 30—26, 8—12, 22—18, 6—9, and now if 25—22 or 26—22 move 11—16.

O

(51) 10—14, 23—19, 11—16

10—14	30—26
23—19	1—6
11—16ᴬ	19—15
26—23ᴮ	10—19
6—10ᶜ	24—15

A Most mid-games are equal with White having a slight lead in deciding what choice.

B Also 19—15, 16—19, 22—17, 7—10, 17—13, 3—7, 27—23, 14—17.

C Now 9—14, 23—19, 11—16, 26—23, 6—9. See (36).

(52) 10—14, 23—19, 14—18

10—14	21—17 *B*
23—19	8—11
14—18 *A*	17—13
22—15	9—14
11—18	25—21

A Some interesting complicated mid-games arise with White usually having the upper hand but Black also has winning chances.

B 26—22, 7—11, 22—15, 11—18, 21—17.

○

(53) 10—14, 24—19, 6—10

10—14	28—24
24—19	13—22
6—10 *A*	25—9
22—17 *B*	5—14
9—13 *C*	29—25

A Strong for White.

B Now 9—14, 22—17, 6—9, 24—19. See opening (27).

C Equal choice is 11—15, 17—13, 15—24, 13—6, 2—9, 28—19, 8—11, 25—22, 11—15.

○

(54) 10—14, 24—19, 7—10

10—14	22—18
24—19	3—7
7—10 *A*	18—9
28—24 *B*	5—14
9—13	25—22

A Leads to a strong White game with much exploration due on this three mover.

B 22—17, 9—13, 27—24, 13—22, 25—9, 5—14.

(55) 10—14, 24—19, 11—16

10—14	22—17
24—19	9—13
11—16 A	26—22
28—24 B,C	5—9
7—10	30—26

A White best but many consider the opening even.

B Equal choice is 22—18, 8—11, 25—22 (26—22, 16—20), 4—8, 22—17 (28—24, 16—20, 30—25, 11—16, 22—17, 7—10), 9—13, 18—9, 13—22, 26—17, 6—22, 30—26, 5—9, 26—17, 9—14. Don't confuse this position with 10—14, 22—18, 11—16, 25—22, 16—20, 24—19, 8—11, 22—17, 9—13, 17—10, 6—22, 26—17, 13—22, 30—26, 5—9, 26—17, now 9—13 must be made.

C Be prepared for 22—17, 14—18, 23—14, 9—18, now 19—15 or 25—22. This position is a secondary line of 10—14, 22—17, 14—18. See (46).

○

(56) 10—14, 24—19, 14—18

10—14	22—15
24—19	11—18
14—18 A	21—17 B
23—14	8—11
9—18	17—13

A Black makes an early thrust with this move putting him slightly on the defensive. After pounding by the champs and analysts this won't be one of real "tuff" openings.

B Now 10—15, 21—17, 15—18, 23—14, 9—18, 22—15, 11—18, 24—19. See (66).

(57) 10—14, 24—20, 6—10

10—14	18—11
24—20	8—15
6—10 A	28—24
22—18	1—6
11—15	23—19 B

A White corrals the advantage but both sides can keep the game confining.

B Continue 9—13, 25—22, 6—9, 29—25, 4—8. Now an Edinburgh position from 9—13, 22—18, 6—9, 25—22, 11—15, 18—11, 8—15, 24—20, 4—8, 28—24, 1—6, 23—19, 9—14, 29—25, 6—9. See (4).

○

(58) 10—14, 24—20, 7—10

10—14	20—11
24—20	8—22
7—10 A	25—18
22—18 B	4—8
11—16 C	28—24

A A powerful position for White and a popular stamping ground for exploring new lines.

B Text is best but strong games develop from 28—24 and 27—24.

C 10—15 is the accepted draw, but not withstanding this fact Wiswell, Bobby Martin and I believe 11—16 tenable and will prove an easier to handle formation. Recently Bobby Martin has brought out some startling play substantiating Black's drawing possibilities.

(59) 10—14, 24—20, 11—15

10—14	26—10 C
24—20	7—14
11—15 A	25—22
22—18 B	8—11
15—22	29—25

A Leading to an even game on most developments.

B 28—24, 8—11, is a line from the Ayrshire Lassie: 11—15, 24—20, 8—11, 28—24, 10—14. See (102).

C Another choice is 25—18, 6—10 D, 26—22, 8—11, 27—24. There is more elasticity in the 26—10 jump than in 25—18. The trunk leads to an open game and a crossboard performer has more scope in handling this type of formation. It will be noted that White releases an apex piece (26) but Black must do likewise (6 or 7).

D Or 12—16.

O

(60) 10—14, 24—20, 11—16

10—14	28—24 B
24—20	6—10
11—16 A	22—17 C,D
20—11	4—8
8—15	17—13 E

A White leads the attack but the Black game is solid. Outside of a few strong lines for White the position tends to develop into an almost even mid-game structure with only a slight pull for White advantage.

B Equal is 22—18, 15—22, 25—18, 6—10, 29—25, 4—8, 25—22, 8—11, 28—24, 1—6, 24—20, 11—16 (published play goes 9—13), 20—11, 7—16, 18—15, 14—18, 22—17, 18—22, 17—13, 22—25, 21—17, 25—29, 3—7, 31—27, 7—10, 11—8.

C 22—18 can also be made.

D If 24—20, 1—6, 22—18, 15—22, 25—18, 3—8.—A. J. Mantell.

E Continue 1—6, 23—19, 15—18, 26—23 (if 24—20 be sure to move 18—23), 8—11, 24—20, 11—15 (the last two Black moves are important), 32—28, 15—24, 28—19, 3—8, 30—26, 14—17, 21—14, 10—17, 23—14, 9—18. Same as a Grover-Long game in the finals of the American championship at Flint, Michigan, in 1939. The game continued into a drawn result, with Mr. Long playing White against me.

○

(61) 10—14, 24—20, 14—18

10—14	23—14
24—20	9—18
14—18*A*	21—17*B*
22—15	8—11
11—18	17—13*C*

A White is best.

B Now the same as 10—15, 21—17, 15—18, 22—15, 11—18, 23—14, 9—18, 24—20. See (66).

C 17—14 is an alternative move and also arises from 11—15, 22—17, 15—18, 23—14, 9—18, 24—20, 8—11, 17—14, 10—17, 21—14. See (90). Also continue after 17—13 at *C* 7—10, 25—21, 10—14, 29—25, 4—8, 28—24, 3—7, 24—19, 6—10, 13—9, 18—23, 27—18, 14—23, 25—22, 5—14, 22—18, 23—27. Maurice Chamberlee.

(62) 10—15, 21—17, 6—10

10—15	23—14
21—17	10—17
6—10A	22—13
17—14B	1—6C
9—18	25—21

A White has an advantage with many crossboard chances arising for both sides.

B Often chosen for a forcing line and well known is 17—13, 1—6, 23—19, 11—16, usually arising from 10—15, 23—19, 6—10, 22—17, 1—6, 25—22, 11—16 giving Black the choice but considered an even game. (67, 78)

C Popular is 12—16, also.

○

(63) 10—15, 21—17, 7—10

10—15	22—13
21—17	11—16D
7—10A	23—19E
17—14B	16—23
10—17C	26—10

A Probably the weakest of all three-move openings for Black. Although a multitude of play has been worked out on this game there is still a lingering doubt whether Black has a tenable game.

B The power.

C 9—18 is given up as a loser. Most of the analysts have neglected this jump majoring on the 10—17 take so perhaps a workable line might be ironed out. Finding a draw on this jump would save the player countless defenses that must be known, at least temporarily until the experts hammered new kinks into the line.

D Only accepted move to draw. 3—7 goes out by 25—21. For a long time 9—14 was thought to have drawn, but consistent poundings by all of the fraternity proved the undoing. See (105).

E 25—22, 24—19, 24—20 require careful

handling by Black and 23—18 is a good secondary choice.

○

(64) 10—15, 21—17, 9—13

10—15	24—19 *B*
21—17	15—24
9—13 *A*	28—19
17—14	6—9
11—16	22—18 *C*

A Another three mover giving White dynamite attacks.

B Prepare for 22—17, 13—22, 25—11, 8—15, 24—19, 15—24, 27—11, 7—16, 23—18, 4—8, 29—25, 8—11, 28—24, 2—7. This variation should be remembered as it can arise from other openings. 10—15, 22—17, 9—13, 17—14, 11—16, 21—17, etc. Also 11—15, 22—17, 15—19, 24—15, 10—19, 23—16, 12—19, 25—22, 8—11, 22—18, 9—14, 18—9, 6—22, 26—17, 11—15, 29—25, 4—8, 25—22, 5—9, 31—26 is the same with the colors reversed. See (69, 91).

C Continue from A. J. Mantell's play: 8—11, 25—22, 16—20, 29—25, 11—16, 19—15, 16—19, 23—16, 12—19, 32—28, 4—8, 15—10, 8—12, 25—21, 19—23, 26—19, 2—6, 28—24, 6—15, 19—10, 13—17, 22—6, 5—9, 14—5, 7—32, 6—2, 20—27, 31—24, and now 12—16 or 32—27 draws.

○

(65) 10—15, 21—17, 11—16

10—15	22—18 *B*
21—17	15—22
11—16 *A*	25—18
17—13	8—11
16—20	29—25

A White has strong lines at his disposal.

B 24—19 is tricky.

139

(66) **10—15, 21—17, 15—18**

10—15	23—14
21—17	9—18
15—18A	24—19B
22—15	8—11
11—18	17—13

A Strong debut for White, but not as deadly as others.

B White has good choice in 24—20 (same as 10—14, 24—20, 14—18, 23—14, 9—18, 22—15, 11—18, 21—17), 8—11, 17—13, 7—10. See (61).

Position is now same as 10—14, 24—19, 14—18, 23—14, 9—18, 22—15, 11—18, 21—17. (56)

O

(67) **10—15, 22—17, 6—10**

10—15	21—14
22—17	9—18
6—10A	23—14
17—14B	1—6
10—17	25—21

A Favors White but not with much sting.

B Necessary to hold the strength. If 23—19, 1—6, 25—22 we have a position arising from 10—15, 23—19, 6—10, 22—17, 1—6, 25—22. (62, 78)

O

(68) **10—15, 22—17, 7—10**

10—15	21—14
22—17	9—18
7—10A	23—14
17—14B	11—16C
10—17	25—22D

A White can develop some rugged positions if Black makes a misstep.

B An even game for Black develops from 25—22, 9—14, 24—20, 3—7, 29—25, 5—9, 17—13, 15—19. See (10—15, 24—20, 7—10). (82)

C This position is important to remember as it can arise from 11—16, 22—17, 7—11, 17—14, 10—17, 21—14, 9—18, 23—14, 11—15; also from 11—16, 22—18, 7—11, 18—14, etc. See (110, 113).

D Now safe enough is 16—19.

(69) **10—15, 22—17, 9—13**

10—15	21—17 C
22—17	13—22
9—13 A	25—11
17—14	8—15
11—16 B	24—19

A Strong for White.

B There is some preference for 15—19, 24—15, 11—18, 23—22, 7—11, 22—15, 11—18, 28—24, 3—7.

C We now have 10—15, 21—17, 9—13, 17—14, 11—16, 22—17. (64, 91)

○

(70) **10—15, 22—17, 11—16**

10—15	25—18
22—17	9—14
11—16 A	18—9
23—18 B	6—22
15—22	26—17

A White has slightly more choice—the games develop into even positions.

B If 25—22, 16—19.

○

(71) **10—15, 22—17, 15—19**

10—15	23—14
22—17	9—18
15—19 A	26—23 B
24—15	6—9
11—18	23—14

A White is again the favorite.

B Better than 17—14, 8—11.

○

(72) **10—15, 22—18, 15—22**

10—15	24—19 B
22—18	11—15
15—22 A	18—11
25—18	8—24
9—13	28—19

A Black has a slight inferior position.

B 29—25, 11—15, 18—11, 8—15, 25—22, 4—8, 23—18, 8—11.

141

(73) 10—15, 23—18, 6—10

10—15	24—19
23—18	15—24
6—10 A	22—6
18—14	1—10
9—18	28—19 B

A Black on the defensive.

B Continue 11—15, 27—24, 15—18 (many prefer 8—11), 31—27, 8—11, 21—17, 18—23, 27—18, 10—14, 17—10, 7—23, 19—15, 11—18, 26—19, 18—23, 25—22, 2—7, 22—18, 7—11, 19—15, 3—7, 15—8, 4—11, 29—25, 7—10, 24—19, 5—9, 25—21, 10—14, 19—15, 11—16, 15—10, 16—19, 10—6, 12—16. *Drawn*—Tom Wiswell.

O

(74) 10—15, 23—18, 7—10

10—15	32—27 B
23—18	15—19
7—10 A	24—15
27—23	10—19
3—7	23—16 C

A An even game, sometimes played under two-move restriction.

B Published play usually went 24—20, 15—19, 23—16, 12—19, 18—15.

C See games 5 and 6 of Grover-Hanson match.

O

(75) 10—15, 23—18, 9—14

10—15	26—23 B
23—18	15—18
9—14 A	22—15
18—9	11—18
5—14	21—17

A White develops a strong game.

B Transposing into 9—14, 22—18, 10—15, 18—9, 5—14, 26—22. See (31).

142

(76) 10—15, 23—18, 11—16

10—15	22—18 B
23—18	15—22
11—16 A	25—18
18—11	16—20
8—15	29—25

A White has a variety of choice. On most variations Black must come to a key position where a star move will clear his position and lead to clear sailing.

B White's strength.

○

(77) 10—15, 23—18, 12—16

10—15	23—16
23—18	11—20
12—16 A	18—11
26—23 B	8—15
16—19	22—18

A Often played under the Two-Move Restriction and gives White a slight pull.

B A popular choice. Another line is 21—17, 9—13, 17—14, 16—19, 24—20, 6—9, 27—24, 1—6. See (24).

○

(78) 10—15, 23—19, 6—10

10—15	25—22
23—19	11—16
6—10 A	17—13
22—17 B	16—23
1—6	26—19

A Almost an even game with Black having the slight edge.

B Can arise from 10—15, 22—17, 6—10, 23—19: but only a secondary choice for that opening. (62, 67)

○

(79) 10—15, 23—19, 7—10

10—15	25—18
23—19	9—14
7—10 A	18—9
22—18 B	5—14
15—22	27—23

A An even game.

B The move simplifies matters for White, cutting out much of Black choice had he elected the alternate move 22—17. See (100).

143

(80) 10—15, 24—19, 15—24

10—15	22—18 C
24—19	11—15
15—24 A	18—11
28—19	8—24
6—10 B	27—20

A Black has the edge.

B Equal would be 9—14, 22—18, 7—10.

C Popular and played often is 22—17, 9—14, 25—22, 11—15, 27—24, 8—11, 23—18, 14—23, 17—14, 10—17, 21—14, 7—10.

○

(81) 10—15, 24—20, 6—10

10—15	23—19
24—20	15—18
6—10 A	22—15
28—24	11—18
1—6	32—28 B

A Present play rates the opening even. Some published games suggest White is strong, others Black. The surface is only scratched on this opening.

B Some suggest 26—22, 7—11, 22—15, 11—18, 32—28.

○

(82) 10—15, 24—20, 7—10

10—15	25—22
24—20	3—7
7—10 A	29—25
22—17 B	5—9
9—14	17—13 C

A I classify this game even.

B Some prefer going into the 3—8 Ayshire Lassie opening by 28—24, 3—7, 23—19 (11—15, 24—20, 8—11, 28—24, 3—8, 23—19) favorable for Black. See (102).

C Strickland moved 15—19, 23—16, 12—19, 22—17 D, 11—15, 20—16, 8—12, 27—24, 4—8, 31—27, 7—11, 16—7, 2—11, 27—23, 11—16, 25—22, 1—5, 32—27. White can force this position from 10—15, 22—17, 7—10, 25—22 (17—14 is better) 9—14, 24—20, 3—7, 29—25, 5—9, 17—13, 15—19, etc. See (68).

D If 20—16, 11—20, 22—17, 7—11.

144

(83) 10—15, 24—20, 15—19

10—15	27—24
24—20	7—10
15—19 A	24—15
23—16	10—19
12—19	21—17 B

A Black has the advantage but the game is well known. Under two move 10—15, 24—20, Black usually replied 15—19 and in matches and tourneys countless games were played over and over again.

B Continue 11—15, 32—27, 6—10, 17—14, 9—18, 26—23, 19—26, 30—7, 3—10. The line invariably taken in the old two move style of play.

◯

(84) 11—15, 21—17, 8—11

11—15	25—21
21—17	9—14
8—11 A	24—19
17—13	15—24
11—16 B	28—19

A Considered even.

B 9—14, 25—21, 11—16 would be the same as trunk in a few moves. This game has the characteristics of the Pioneer. See (29, 86, 108).

◯

(85) 11—15, 21—17, 9—13

11—15	30—25 C
21—17	4—8
9—13 A	24—19
25—21	15—24
8—11 B	28—19 D

A Called the Switcher and is strong for Black.

B 5—9 and 6—9 run into the 9—13, 21—17, 5—9 and the 9—13, 21—17, 6—9 openings. See opening (1) and (2).

C The majority of experts favor the old standby 17—14, 10—17, 21—14, 6—10, 22—17—a somewhat safer line but the text has been my favorite. A line coming into favor is 24—19.

D Now if 11—15, 17—14 is correct and if 11—16, 22—18.

(86) 11—15, 21—17, 9—14

11—15	17—13
21—17	11—16C
9—14A	24—19
25—21B	15—24
8—11	28—19

A Considered an even opening.

B 15—19 is the favorite of many players and forms the Double Corner Dyke.

C Now into a well known Pioneer arising from many openings. See (29, 84, 108).

○

(87) 11—15, 21—17, 15—19

11—15	23—16
21—17	12—19
15—19A	27—24B
24—15	7—10
10—19	24—15

A Dykeing this opening is strong for White.

B The move now exploited—also 22—18, 7—10.

○

(88) 11—15, 22—17, 8—11

11—15	24—20
22—17	16—23
8—11A	27—11
23—19	7—16
11—16B	20—11C

A Positions arising slightly favor Black who has most of the choice to make.

B Leads to simplicity but Black is best. Other moves include any of the following—4—8, 3—8, 15—18, 9—14 and 9—13 all good. (28, 98)

C Now 3—7, 28—24 (11—8 is sound enough but all the players tread away from it), 7—16, 24—20.

146

(89) 11—15, 22—17, 9—13

11—15	25—11
22—17	8—15
9—13 A	21—17
24—20 B	5—9
13—22	17—13

A An even game.

B Now a transposition of 9—13, 24—20, 11—15, 22—17. (25)

○

(90) 11—15, 22—17, 15—18

11—15	24—20 B
22—17	8—11
15—18 A	17—14
23—14	10—17
9—18	21—14 C

A White has the initiative and the better position.

B 26—23, 6—9, 23—14, 9—18, 30—26, 1—6.

C This position is the same as 10—14, 24—20, 14—18, 22—15, 11—18, 23—14, 9—18, 21—17, 8—11, 17—14. (61)

○

(91) 11—15, 22—17, 15—19

11—15	23—16
22—17	12—19
15—19 A	25—22 B
24—15	8—11
10—19	27—23 C

A This game is even. See (26). Also (64, 69).

B 9—14 (second choice) is (28, 29, 108). Some prefer the older line 30—25 but the modern players accept the text. Continue after 27—23, 4—8, simplifies the position but 11—16, 29—25, 9—13, 17—14, 6—9, 31—27, 9—18, 23—14, 4—8, is tricky. Continue: 4—8, 23—16, 11—20, 22—18, 8—11, 32—27. See (26).

147

(92) 11—15, 22—18, 15—22

11—15	29—25
22—18	4—8
15—22 A	24—20
25—18	12—16 C
8—11 B	26—22 D

A Reams of play has been published on this opening. Called the Single Corner Black has the choice and a slightly superior game. See (19).

B Also 10—14 or 12—16.

C 10—15, 25—22.

D Now 9—13.

○

(93) 11—15, 23—18, 8—11

11—15	22—17 C
23—18	15—22
8—11 A	17—10
27—23	6—15
10—14 B	25—18 D

A Although White is inferior he can secure many wins. Black forces the opening moves, then White usually decides the route. One of my favorite openings in my exhibitions and I find White unusually tricky.

B Considered strong but the game is open and White only needs a few variations on it to secure his draw. Black usually avoids the line to keep it more complicated. Good moves are 4—8, 23—19, and now 9—14 or 10—14.

C 23—19 is considered safer but 22—17 avoids certain strong lines and narrows the Black attacks.

D The line adopted by the great Ginsberg in his historic match with the late Sam Gonotsky.

(94) 11—15, 23—18, 9—14

11—15	22—18
23—18	14—23 C
9—14 A	27—11
18—11 B	7—16
8—15	25—22

A Forms the Cross Choice opening, an even game.

B Not quite as good is 18—9, 5—14, 22—17, 8—11, 25—22.

C Quoting from a game I reviewed in "Let's Play Checkers"—15—22 is more popular because of the natural and easy-going style of lines of play involved, plus the possibilities of frequent duplications of positions that occur in mid games of other openings. In many important encounters this 14—23 jump has been taken. Both sides in this game have a temporary weakness as pieces 7 and 27 are removed from the board. This move gives greater scope than the 15—22 jump and is favored by many experts, and by those who like to mix the game to get their opponents off the book lanes.

○

(95) 11—15, 23—18, 10—14

11—15	26—23 B
23—18	6—10
10—14 A	22—17
18—11	4—8
8—15	23—19 C

A Favors White but wins prevail for both sides.

B Crops up regular from 10—14, 22—18, 11—15, 18—11, 8—15, 26—22. See (48).

C Regular continuation is 8—11, 17—13, 1—6, 25—22, now 14—17 or 14—18 is a hard draw. Lieber and Rubin worked on 7—11 after 23—19 and seemed to get a better game for Black than previous play (8—11).

149

11—15	24—20
23—18	9—14 B
12—16 A	20—11
18—11	7—16
8—15	22—18

A White has a powerful position.

B There is much speculation for Black's best reply. Other choice includes 16—19 and 7—11. Ryan favors 7—11 but the majority of experts to date cling to 9—14. These include Long, Hanson, Wiswell and myself. An unorthodox development occurs with 7—11.

O

(97) 11—15, 23—18, 15—19

11—15	22—17 B
23—18	12—16
15—19 A	17—14
24—15	7—11
10—19	27—24 C

A Black must be on the defensive.

B 27—24, 7—10, 24—15, 10—19, 32—27, 3—7, 27—24, 7—10, 24—15, 10—19, 31—27, 2—7.

C The next few moves are important: 11—15, 18—11, 8—15, 14—10, 9—14, 24—20, (if 25—22, 5—9) 5—9, 20—11, 19—23, 26—19, 15—24, 28—19, 6—24, 25—22, 24—28, 30—26, 1—6.

O

(98) 11—15, 23—19, 8—11

11—15	24—20
23—19	16—23
8—11 A	27—11
22—17 B	7—16
11—16 C	20—11

A Black has most of the choice and also superior in many variations.

B Ryan favors the weaker but far more restrictive 22—18. Trunk is now same as 11—15, 22—17, 8—11, 23—19. (See 28, 100).

C Almost any other move is good but 11—16 is my line. See (88)

(99) 11—15, 23—19, 9—13

11—15	15—22
23—19	25—18
9—13 A	10—14 B
11—15	18—9
22—18	5—14

A Black and White are on a par.

B More complicated and sometimes preferred is 7—11, 19—15 C, 10—19, 24—15, 12—16, 29—25, 6—9, 26—23, 9—14.

C My choice for simplification (Sometimes the score tends to decide what type of game we prefer—a game down, mix her up; a game up, simplify) is 27—23, 10—15.

○

(100) 11—15, 23—19, 9—14

11—15	22—18
23—19	15—22
9—14 A	25—9
27—23 B	5—14
8—11 C	29—25 D

A White is restricted.

B 22—17 offers a better mid game but opens up too many avenues for Black. Text keeps the game on a narrower path. This 27—23 move forms the Defiance. See (28, 35, 79, 98).

C If 5—9, 22—18, 15—22, 25—18, 7—11, 19—15 (or 26—22). See (35, 38).

D. The Defiance is apt to arise from many other openings sometimes with colors reversed.

○

(101) 11—15, 24—19, 15—24

11—15	22—18
24—19	10—14 B
15—24 A	25—22
28—19	6—10
8—11	29—25

A Black is on the offensive but White has winning chances also. The game is a favorite of Newell Banks. Anyone knowing all the weaknesses of many openings can control the opponent and snare many wins. This opening is called the Second Double Corner.

B Easier going is 9–14, 18–9, 5–14, 25–22. Black has a few tricks to play for on this line. See (39).

○

(102) 11–15, 24–20, 8–11

11–15	23–19
24–20	15–18
8–11 A	22–15
28–24 B	11–18
4–8 C	26–22

A Black has most of the option.

B Although 11–15, 24–20 is called the Ayrshire Lassie, 28–24 marks the characteristic of the opening.

C If 3–8, 23–19, 9–14, 26–23, 5–9, 22–17, 1–5, 30–26, 11–16 (9–13, 32–28) 20–11, 7–16, 25–22. See (82).

○

(103) 11–15, 24–20, 12–16

11–15	22–18 B
24–20	15–22
12–16 A	25–18
20–11	8–11
7–16	29–25 C

A White develops best.

B Black relinquishes the center giving White command.

C If 18–14, 10–17, 21–14, 9–18, 23–14, 6–9.

○

(104) 11–15, 24–20, 15–18

11–15	22–15
24–20	10–19
15–18 A	25–22
23–14 B	5–9
9–18	21–17

A Opinion varies on the strength of this opening. White should have some leeway, I believe.

B More often chosen as 22–15, 10–19, 23–16, 12–19, 25–22, 7–10, 22–18.

152

(105) 11–16, 21–17, 7–11

11–16	22–13
21–17	11–15 *B*
7–11 *A*	23–19
17–14	16–23
10–17	26–10

A In conjunction with 10–15, 21–17, 7–10 reputed to offer White his best opportunity of all the openings.

B Now same as 10–15, 21–17, 7–10, 17–14. (63)

O

(106) 11–16, 21–17, 8–11

11–16	22–13
21–17	4–8
8–11 *A*	24–19
17–14 *B*	16–20
10–17	25–22 *C*

A Black must evince some careful manipulation of his pieces, especially in the early mid-game.

B The hidden power.

C A careful continuation must still be made—continue: 11–16, 29–25, 7–10, 22–17 *D*, 10–14. Oliver Mauro thrashed out some fine play on the above after many players and analysts including myself skipped over this screwball looking move.

D 25–21, 3–7, 22–17, 8–11, 26–22, 11–15, 28–24, 9–14—Mauro.

O

(107) 11–16, 21–17, 9–13

11–16	23–18
21–17	10–15 *B*
9–13 *A*	18–11
25–21	8–15
5–9	24–19

A An even game and often a rest game for the experts.

B If 1–5, 27–23, 16–19, 23–16, 12–19, 24–15, 10–19, 17–14.

(108) 11—16, 21—17, 9—14

11—16	24—15
21—17	10—19
9—14 A	17—10
25—21 B	6—15
16—19 C	23—16

A Neither side has an advantage but both have possibilities to transpose into other openings.

B Best, and same as 9—14, 22—17, 11—16, 25—22. See (29, 84, 86).

C Option would be 8—11, running into the Pioneer. The 16—19 bust is called the Double Corner Dyke and can be formed from 9—14, 22—17, 11—15 (or 11—16), 25—21, 16—19. Also 11—15, 22—17, 15—19, 24—15, 10—19, 23—16, 12—19, 25—22, 9—14 will run into the opening shortly. See (28, 29, 91)

O

(109) 11—16, 21—17, 16—20

11—16	29—25 B
21—17	9—14
16—20 A	17—13
25—21	11—15
8—11	24—19

A Boundless offerings to change the channels are offered both sides. The game is considered equal.

B 22—18, 9—14 is another line.

O

(110) 11—16, 22—17, 7—11

11—16	21—14
22—17	9—18
7—11 A	23—14
17—14 B	11—15 C
10—17	25—22

A After the key moves are made by Black in the opening and mid-game he should have almost clear sailing.

B Check with 11—16, 22—18, 7—11, 18—14—same. See (113).

C Transposed into 10—15, 22—17, 7—10, 17—14, 10—17, 21—14, 9—18, 23—14, 11—16. See (68).

(111) 11-16, 22-17, 8-11

11-16	23-14	A Offers White the selection and the
22-17	10-17	better game.
8-11	21-14	B The offensive move, 25-22 or 24-19
17-14B	16-20	will run into the Pioneer. See (29, etc.).
9-18	25-22	Now the same as 11-16, 22-18, 8-11,
		17-14 (114)

O

(112) 11-16, 22-17, 16-20

11-16	23-14	A White has the initiative.
22-17	10-17	B Often arises from 11-16, 22-18,
16-20A	21-14	16-20, 18-14, 9-18, 23-14, 10-17,
17-14	8-11B	21-14, 8-11. (116)
9-18	25-22	

O

(113) 11-16, 22-18, 7-11

11-16	21-14	A Black plays cautiously in the opening
22-18	9-18	and mid-game and can get almost an even
7-11A	23-14	ending in most variations—but the fight is
18-14B	11-15C	an uphill one.
10-17	25-22	B If 24-19, we have 11-16, 24-19,

7-11, 22-18. (122) At B 25-22 is an equal
choice, followed by 3-7, 29-25, 16-19,
23-16, 12-19, 24-15, 10-19, 21-17, 9-13,
17-14 (if 25-21, 6-10) 6-10. At B position arises from 11-16, 22-17, 7-11,
17-14 (110)
C Same as 10-15, 22-17, 7-10, 17-14,
10-17, 21-14, 9-18, 23-14, 11-16. (68)

(114) 11—16, 22—18, 8—11

11—16	22—17
22—18	9—14
8—11 A	18—9
25—22 B	5—14
16—20 C	29—25 D

A Black must do the defending on White's choosing.

B 18—14 is 11—16, 22—17, 8—11, 17—14.

C Now 11—16, 22—18, 16—20, 25—22, 8—11. (111 and 116)

D Another Pioneer.

○

(115) 11—16, 22—18, 16—19

11—16	24—15
22—18	10—19
16—19 A	25—22
23—16	9—14
12—19	18—9 B

A White has a good attack.

B This arises via: 9—14, 22—18, 11—16, 18—9, 5—14, 25—22, 16—19, 24—15, 10—19, 23—16, 12—19.

○

(116) 11—16, 22—18, 16—20

11—16	23—14
22—18	10—17
16—20 A	21—14
18—14 B	8—11
9—18	25—22

A White slightly best.

B Same as 11—16, 22—17, 16—20, 17—14. See (112). White can vary by 24—19, 8—11, 25—22, 4—8, 22—17, 9—14, 18—9— Pioneer.

○

(117) 11—16, 23—18, 7—11

11—16	22—15
23—18	10—19
7—11 A	24—15
18—15 B	3—7
11—18	25—22

A Black is vulnerable to the White attacks if he starts off wrong.

B If 26—23, 3—7 is correct.

156

(118) 11—16, 23—18, 8—11

11—16	22—8
23—18	4—11
8—11 A	25—22
18—14 B	16—20
9—18	26—23

A White has an inconsiderable benefit of position.

B 26—23, 4—8, 24—19, 16—20, 22—17, 9—14.

○

(119) 11—16, 23—18, 9—14

11—16	22—17 B
23—18	8—11
9—14 A	25—22
18—9	16—20
5—14	26—23 C

A Although considered an even opening, I believe White has selection and an edge.

B Alternate 24—19 is favorable also.

C Now 11—15, 29—25 is an old Pioneer position, a favorite of Louis Ginsberg: 9—14, 22—17, 11—16, 25—22, 8—11, 22—18, 16—20, 18—9, 5—14, 29—25, 11—15, 26—22 (or White can move 25—22, or 24—19 as equal choices for Pioneer). See (29, etc.)

○

(120) 11—16, 23—18, 10—14

11—16	24—19
23—18	8—11
10—14 A	30—26
26—23	3—7 B
7—10	28—24

A Develops into an even game, White having selections.

B If 16—20, 22—17, 11—16, 26—22, 9—13, 18—9, 5—14.

○

(121) 11—16, 23—18, 16—20

11—16	18—15 B
23—18	7—10
16—20 A	22—17
24—19	9—13
10—14	27—23

A Black can be drawn into an ending which requires careful tactics to draw. White also has leeway. Can easily be run into other openings. See (124).

B If 26—23, 8—11, 22—17, 7—10, 28—24.

157

(122) 11—16, 24—19, 7—11

11—16	25—22 B
24—19	11—15
7—11 A	18—11
22—18	8—24
3—7	28—19

A A difficult opening to handle unless familiar with the kinks and then White has some strength. In 11—16, 22—18, 7—11, White can run this opening into text but 18—14 or 25—22 is superior. (113)

B 28—24, 9—14, 18—9, 5—14, 26—22, 11—15, 22—18, 15—22, 25—9, 6—13, 29—25, 16—20.

○

(123) 11—16, 24—19, 8—11

11—16	25—22 C
24—19	7—10
8—11 A	27—24
22—18	16—20
10—14 B	19—16

A Reams of published data is offered in various text books on this opening. Black gives his opponent the right of way on many variations but he can also lead at various stages. White is a slight favorite.

B Known as the Paisley and its characteristics must be known.

C 26—22, 16—20, 22—17, 7—10, 30—26, 11—16, 26—22, 9—13 is often played.

○

(124) 11—16, 24—19, 16—20

11—16	18—15
24—19	7—10
16—20 A	22—17
23—18 B	9—13
10—14	27—23

A Partial to White.

B Now 11—16, 23—18, 16—20, 24—19. See (121). Another usual line is 22—18, 10—14, 25—22, 8—11, 22—17, 9—13. Many of the 11—16, 24—19 and 11—16, 22—18 openings are akin to one another on certain variations.

(125) 11—16, 24—20, 16—19

11—16	22—18
24—20	9—14 _B_
16—19 _A_	18—9
23—16	5—14
12—19	25—22

_A_ Ranked an even opening, with an abundance of published play on hand.

_B_ 10—14 can complicate matters. White might play for simplification by 18—15, 14—18, 27—23 (21—17 leads to involved play), 18—27, 32—16, 7—10, 16—12, 10—19, 31—27, 19—23, 27—18, 3—7, 12—3, 9—13, 3—10, 6—31, 30—26 to a draw.

O

(126) 12—16, 21—17, 9—13

12—16	20—11
21—17	7—16
9—13 _A_	25—21
24—20 _B_	5—9
11—15	23—18

_A_ The strength is divided with White having a few more chances for making the route.

_B_ Against 25—21 either 5—9 or 16—19 is satisfactory.

O

(127) 12—16, 21—17, 9—14

12—16	23—16
21—17	11—20
9—14 _A_	25—21
17—13 _B_	8—11
16—19	22—17

_A_ An even game with good crossboard opportunities for either player. Even though this game was played in the two move era there is still plenty of room for scope.

_B_ If 25—21, 16—19, 24—15. A good mixer is 24—19, 14—21, 19—12, 11—16, 22—17, 8—11, 25—22.

12—16	23—16
21—17	11—20
16—19 A	25—21
24—15	8—11
10—19	22—18 B

A Some textbooks pass over lightly the White strength. White has a tremendous advantage in my opinion unless it is my voodoo opening. At the 10th tourney in the finals of the American Championship I lost on this opening to Long. In my match with Ginsberg this was the only game I lost to him. Ginsberg lost to Hunt in the 7th Tourney from a transposition to this opening.

B This position arises via: 12—16, 22—17, 16—19, 24—15, 10—19 (11—18 might be better), 23—16, 11—20, 25—22, 8—11, 22—18. The Ginsberg-Hunt game ran like this: 12—16, 22—18, 16—19, 24—15, 10—19, 23—16, 11—20, 25—22, 8—11, 22—17. Also see Note B of 12—16, 22—18, 16—19. See (130, 132).

○

12—16	24—19
21—17	15—24
16—20 A	28—19
17—13 B	8—11
11—15	22—18

A White selects the lines in most variations.

B 17—14 is an alternate move followed by 9—18 (or 10—17), 23—14, 10—17, 22—13, 11—15.

(130) 12—16, 22—17, 16—19

12—16	23—14
22—17	9—18
16—19 A	26—23
24—15	6—9
11—18 B	23—14

A Black treads a narrow lane.

B Jumping 10—19 leads to the 12—16, 21—17, 16—19 and 12—16, 22—18, 16—19 openings. See Note B: 12—16, 22—18, 16—19. See (128, 132).

○

(131) 12—16, 22—17, 16—20

12—16	18—11
22—17	8—15
16—20 A	17—13
23—18 B	4—8
11—15	25—22

A An even game.

B Modern players favor 17—14, 9—18, 23—14, 10—17, 21—14, 6—9, 26—23, or 24—19. See (133).

○

(132) 12—16, 22—18, 16—19

12—16	23—16
22—18	11—20
16—19 A	25—22
24—15	8—11 B
10—19	22—17 C

A A powerhouse for White unless well known by the defense.

B Long's adoption is 6—10, 22—17, 1—6, 17—13, 8—11, 29—25, 10—15, 25—22, 7—10, 26—23, 3—7, 28—24, 4—8, 23—19, 8—12, 27—23 (if 31—26, 11—16) 20—27, 31—24, 9—14. This should lead to a popular defense of this opening. This can arise from three openings. See Note C. See (128, 130).

C Now same as 12—16, 21—17, 16—19 and 12—16, 22—17, 16—19. The continued defense is 9—14, 18—9, 6—22 (some prefer 5—14, 17—10, 7—14), 26—17, 5—9, 29—25, 11—15, 25—22, 4—8, 30—26, 8—11, 17—13, 9—14, 26—23, 7—10, 23—19, 15—24, 28—19, 11—15, 32—28, 15—24, 28—19, 2—6, 27—23, 10—15.

161

(133) 12—16, 22—18, 16—20

12—16	22—17	A White is slightly best.
22—18	9—14	B Or 18—14. See (131).
16—20 A	18—9	
25—22 B	5—14	
8—12	29—25	

○

(134) 12—16, 23—18, 16—19

12—16	27—24 B
23—18	7—10
16—19 A	24—15
24—15	10—19
10—19	21—17

A The pull is with White.

B If 21—17, 11—15, 18—11, 8—15, 27—23, 4—8, 23—16, 8—12, 22—18, 15—22, 25—18, 12—19, 17—13, 9—14.

○

(135) 12—16, 23—18, 16—20

12—16	22—17
23—18	9—14
16—20 A	18—9
26—23 B	5—14
8—12	25—22 C

A White has plentiful of choice.

B 24—19, 11—15, 18—11, 8—24, 28—19, 9—14, 26—23.

C A regular Pioneer formation.

○

(136) 12—16, 24—19, 16—20

12—16	26—23
24—19	8—12
16—20 A	22—17
23—18 B	7—10
10—14	30—26 C

A Most of the selection of the lines are in the control by White.

B 22—17 and 22—18 can also be made.

C A position arriving from many 11—16 and 12—16 openings.

162

(137) 12-16, 24-20, 8-12

12-16	24-19c	A The preference is for White.
11-15	24-20	
		B If 9-14, 22-17 (22-18, 3-8), 3-8,
8-12A	20-11	26-22, 11-15, 20-11, 7-16, 24-20.
28-24	15-24	
		C 22-18, 16-19, 24-15, 10-19, 23-16,
8-8B	27-20	12-19, 25-22, 9-14. If 23-18 at Note C
		move 9-13.
		D And 7-16.

The ABC of Problem Composing

EVERY player is a problem composer in embryo, but he seldom knows how to go about creating a problem. He is like the budding author who aspires to write the great American novel but does not know just how to begin.

A good problemist must have imagination, analytical ability, sound positional judgment, perseverance in the face of many disappointments, and, what is most important of all, originality of conception. The works of Slocum, Heffner, Dalumi and Nelson all show a great wealth of varied and assorted themes. The successful problemist *must* have an idea to start with.

It is said that every novel is founded on one of six or seven basic plots, and to a certain extent this is also true of checker problems. Yet, just as tens of thousands of *different* stories have been written around these basic plots, so, too, have thousands of fine problem settings been published around the *basic ideas*—the stroke, the smother, the waiting move, the captive Cossack, the fugitive King, and so on. So to the student problemist I would say, first you must have an idea, an original one if possible, but an idea, anyway.

Your next task will be to develop the proper setting for your brain-child, and there your woes and difficulties will begin, as any veteran composer can attest. It is necessary to avoid duals and yet maintain the terms of the problem. To do this and satisfactorily conceal the idea from the solver is no easy task. Many a composer has suffered heart-break by having a beautiful idea but no satisfactory setting with which to embellish it and thus mystify and intrigue the solver.

Slocum's settings, for example, are among the finest of any

164

composer. His ideas are consummately hidden, his solutions not too long or burdensome, and all his problems bear an innocent, natural appearance. I would recommend a close study of Slocum's gems to any budding problem composer. They reveal all the admirable finesse of the composer's art.

The student is cautioned against the use of numerous Kings in his work as they often tend to lend an artificial appearance to the setting. Now and then one may run across a nice problem containing all Kings, but such problems are in a different category entirely.

It is also a good habit for the embryo composer to show his problems to a friend or two before submitting them for publication. This insures against duals and incorrect terms. One cannot always trust his own judgment, no matter how accurate one may be as a rule. We have often seen "duffers" point out simple errors we overlooked in our pardonable zeal and enthusiasm. Remember, a composer who submits many problems with imperfect solutions or incorrect terms soon loses caste among the players. The best composers will err now and then, of course, but the greater they are, the fewer their errors.

Don't try to "turn out" dozens of problems at a time on a mass-production, "assembly line" basis. Many problems published in weekly and monthly periodicals are not worth the paper they are printed on. Such composers are not worthy of the name. *Some problemists are gone but not forgotten; others are forgotten but not gone!* Be sure you are not in the latter group.

It is, of course, sometimes difficult to avoid unintentional plagiarism, but always strive for *originality* and, above all, avoid any intentional "stealing" of settings. If one of your variations runs into a known theme, be frank and say so in your solution and give full credit where due.

An interesting and valuable point to bear in mind is that every game eventually evolves into a problem setting. Be on the alert, therefore, for problem possibilities in all your games. I have seen many players run up beautiful continuations and quickly reset the pieces for a new game, never realizing they had wholly neglected an interesting and perhaps instructive problem setting in the game they had just completed. Such players invariably remind me of the man who slept while traveling, in broad daylight, through the Grand Canyon. I have been able to get as many as half a dozen fine settings from a single game, and this number is small indeed.

Above all, don't get discouraged. The first problem is always the toughest. Don't expect a gem to start off with. Be content with a nice beginner's problem as your initial effort. Depth and true beauty will come with time.

Slocum, Heffner, Dalumi and Nelson (the Four Horsemen) did not attain eminence overnight. Rather their stature and greatness developed slowly with the years, as players the world over came to recognize that the works of these masters were gems of the highest order, elevating their handiwork to the stratosphere of a fine art.

T. W.

166

PROBLEM NO. 1

By TOMMIE WISWELL

BLACK: 2, 19 20, 23 King: 30

WHITE: 28, 31, 32 KING: 21

White to Play and Draw

SOLUTION

NO. 1: 31–27, 30–26, 27–18, 26–22, 18–14 (18–15, 2–7, *Black Wins*), 2–6, 32–27, 22–18, 14–10, 6–15, 21–17, 19–23, 17–14, 18–9 A, 27–11. *Drawn*

A 23–32, 14–23. *White Wins!*

PROBLEM NO. 2

By TOMMIE WISWELL

BLACK: 2, 7, 12, 16, 23

WHITE: 11, 13, 19, 28 KING: 14

White to Play and Win

SOLUTION

NO. 2: 13–9, 16–20 A, 19–16!, 12–19, 14–18!, 7–16 18–27 B, 2–7, 6–9, 7–10, 6–2, 10–14, 2–6, 14–18, 6–10, 18–22 C, 10–15, 22–26, 15–24, 26–30, 27–32, 20–27, 32–23, 30–25, 28–24, 16–20, 23–27, 25–22, 27–32, 20–27, 32–23. *White Wins*

A If 23–27 (or 23–26), 19–15, 16–19, 11–8, 7–11. *White Wins*

B Although White is a man down his superior position is sufficient to force the win.

C 19–23, 10–14. *White Wins*

PROBLEM NO. 3

By TOMMIE WISWELL

BLACK: 3, 6, 10, 14, 28 KING: 29

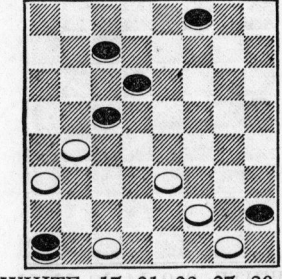

WHITE: 17, 21, 23, 27, 30, 32

White to Play and Win

SOLUTION

NO. 3: 23–19, 14–18, 17–14, 10–17, 21–14, 6–10, 14–7, 3–10, 19–16, 10–14, 16–11, 14–17, 11–7, 17–21, 30–26!A *White Wins*

A Not a very spectacular move but quite effective, never-the-less. Crowning the man on 7 would permit Black to draw. It is the study of endings like this that will give the student the necessary "polish" and distinguish him from the average "woodpusher."

PROBLEM NO. 4

By TOMMIE WISWELL

BLACK: 2, 28 KINGS: 13, 25

WHITE: 6, 9, 14, 19, 22, 32

White to Play and Win

SOLUTION

NO. 4: 22–18, 13–17, 14–10A, 17–14B, 18–15, 14–7, 6–1,
25–22, 1–5, 22–18, 15–11!, 7–23, 32–27, 23–32, 9–6, 2–9,
5–23. *White Wins*

A 6–1, 17–10, 18–15, 10–14, 1–5, 25–22, 19–16, 22–26,
16–12, 26–23, 12–8, 23–19, 15–11, 14–10, 8–3, 19–16, 11–8,
10–6. *Drawn*

B 25–22, 18–14, 22–18, 9–5, 18–9, 10–7, 2–11, 6–2, 17–14,
2–7, 9–6, 7–16, 6–1, 19–15, 14–9, 15–10, 9–6, 10–7, 6–2,
7–3, 2–6 *forms Problem No. 5*

PROBLEM NO. 5

THE D'ORIO-WISWELL POSITION

(A New Standard)

BLACK: 28 KINGS: 1, 6

WHITE: 5, 32 KINGS: 3, 16

White to Play and Win

SOLUTION

NO. 5: 3–7, 6–2, 7–10, 2–6, 10–15, 6–2, 16–19, 2–6, 19–23, 6–9, 15–18, 9–6 (9–13, 18–14W *Wins*), 18–14, 6–2 (6–9, 32–27W *Wins*), 14–17, 2–6, 17–13, 6–2, 23–18, 2–6, 18–14, 6–2, 13–9, 1–6, 5–1, 6–13, 14–9, 13–6, 1–10. *White Wins*

NOTE: The above is the culmination of much play which appeared recently in Emin Elam's "Checkerboard" where many famous critics attempted to upset the terms to Problem No. 4. However, with the aid of the celebrated Julius D'Orio of High Grove, California, the terms were sustained.

171

PROBLEM NO. 6

By FAUSTO DALUMI

BLACK: 2, 20 KING: 27

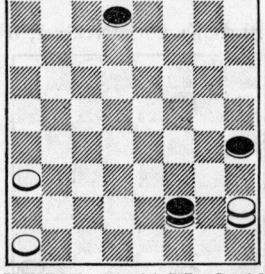

WHITE: 21, 29 KING: 28

White to Play and Draw

SOLUTION

NO. 6: 29–25, 27–23, 25–22, 2–6, 21–17, 6–10, 28–32, 20–24, 17–13, 24–28, 22–17, 23–18, 13–9, 18–14, 9–6, 14–21, 6–2, 21–17, 2–7, etc. *Drawn*

PROBLEM NO. 7

By FAUSTO DALUMI

BLACK: 10, 19, 21 KING: 12

WHITE: 6, 27, 30 KING: 9

White to Play and Win

SOLUTION

NO. 7: 6–2, 12–16, 2–7, 19–23, 27–18, 10–14 7–11, 16–7, 18–15, 14–17, 9–13, 17–22, 13–17, 22–25, 15–10, 7–14, 17–10, 25–29, 10–15, 29–25, 15–18, White Wins

PROBLEM NO. 8

By FAUSTO DALUMI

BLACK: 2, 21, 22 KINGS: 19, 20

WHITE: 30 KINGS: 4, 10, 13

White to Play and Draw

SOLUTION

NO. 8: 13-17, 22-25, 17-22, 4-8, 19-16, 10-14, 2-6, 14-18, 20-24, 18-14, 24-19, 22-17, 19-24, 24-27, 14-17, 27-24, 17-14, 24-19, 22-17, 29-25, 8-3, 16-11, 17-13, 25-22, 14-9, 6-10, 3-7, 11-2, 9-6, 2-9, 13-24. *Drawn*

PROBLEM NO. 9

By FAUSTO DALUMI

BLACK: 3, 8, 12, 21 KINGS: 22, 32

WHITE: 10, 19, 28, 30 KINGS: 1, 2

White to Play and Win

SOLUTION

NO. 9: 1–6, 8–11, 10–7, 3–10, 6–8, 22–18, 2–7, 32–27, 7–11, 18–23, 11–16, 27–24, 16–11, 23–7, 28–19. *White Wins*

PROBLEM NO. 10

By TOM QUINLAN

BLACK: 3 KINGS: 14, 15

WHITE: 22 KINGS: 1, 8, 12

White to Play and Win

SOLUTION

NO. 10: 1–6, 15–19, 12–16, 19–12, 8–11, 3–8, 11–4, 12–16, 4–8, 16–19, 6–2, 19–23, 2–7, 23–26, 8–3, 26–17, 7–10, 14–7, 3–10. *White Wins*

PROBLEM NO. 11

By TOM QUINLAN

BLACK: 3, 5, 7 KING: 25

WHITE: 14, 21, 26, 28, 30

White to Play and Win

SOLUTION

NO. 11: 28-24 3-8, 24-19, 8-11, 21-17, 25-22, 14-10, 7-21, 26-17, 5-9, 17-13, 9-14, 13-9, 14-18. *White Wins*

PROBLEM NO. 12

By PAUL R. SEMPLE

BLACK: 1, 10, 17, 21

WHITE: 13, 23, 25, 30

White to Play and Win

SOLUTION

NO. 12: 13—9, 10—15, 9—5, 1—6, 5—1, 6—10, 1—6, 10—14, 23—19, 15—24, 30—26, 21—30, 6—9, 30—23, 9—20. *White Wins*

PROBLEM NO. 13

By PAUL R. SEMPLE

BLACK: 4, 13 KINGS: 17, 22

WHITE: 16, 26, 27 KINGS: 2, 3

White to Play and Win

SOLUTION

NO. 13: 26–23, 22–26, 23–19, 26–31, 27–24 A, 31–27, 24–20, 27–24, 19–15, 24–19, 2–7, 19–12, 20–16, 12–10, 7–21. *White Wins*

A 27–23, 17–14, 19–15, 31–27, 23–19, 14–18, 15–11, 27–24, 19–15, 24–19. *Drawn*

PROBLEM NO. 14

By BEN BOLAND

BLACK: 24 KINGS: 18, 32

WHITE: 8, 16, 19

Black to Play and Win

SOLUTION

NO. 14: 18—23, 8—3, 32—27, 3—8, 24—28, 8—12, 27—24, 19—15, 23—19, 15—10, 24—20, 16—11, 20—16 and Black wins by the two-for-one via 19—24.

PROBLEM NO. 15

By S. J. PICKERING

BLACK: 1, 6, 13, 19, 23, 27

WHITE: 5, 14, 17, 22, 26, 30

White to Play and Draw

SOLUTION

NO. 15: 14-9, 6-10, 17-14, 10-17, 9-6, 1-10, 30-25, 23-30, 5-1, 30-21, 1-6, 17-26, 6-22. *Drawn.*

A real beauty!

By ARTHUR HIPKINE

BLACK: 2, 4 KINGS: 17, 18

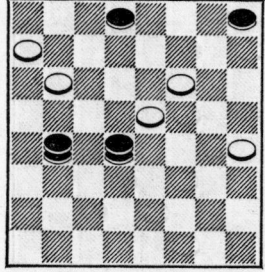

WHITE: 5, 9, 11, 15, 20

White to Play and Draw

SOLUTION

NO. 16: 9–6!!, 2–9, 15–10, 18–15, 11–7, 15–6, 5–1 and regardless of where Black moves he must relinquish the piece.

America's Ten Best Players

A committee of well known players of the great Washington State Checker Association recently made a canvass of sentiment of the players and fans regarding America's foremost players of the day. According to this authoritative body here is how the Nation rates the first ten players on the basis of recent match and tourney records.

THE TOP TEN

NO. 1   William F. Ryan   Mr. Ryan, who is known as "The Bronx Comet," won the 2nd National Tourney of the National Checker Association (held in Tacoma, scene of the Grover-Hanson match), in 1939. He was formerly the World's blindfold champion and is rated by many the finest living authority on three move restriction. He is a tireless promoter and exhibition player and always willing to risk his title and reputation against all worthy opponents.

NO. 2   Kenneth Grover   In 1939 (as runner-up in 10th American Tourney) Grover startled the Checker World by conquering Asa Long and upsetting Long's unbeaten record of 17 years of invincibility. Since then he has also won victories over such stars as Louis Ginsberg, John B. Stiles and Jesse Hanson. There are many who consider Grover the equal of Ryan and as a leading exponent of crossboard play he would prove a fitting opponent for the studious Champion.

NO. 3 Harold Freyer

This lanky New Yorker won third prize at the 10th American Tourney where he succeeded in winning a round from Grover by the score of 1 to 0 and 11 draws. He also won over the great L. M. Lewis in this event. Freyer has often been New York Champion and on three different occasions tied for premier honors in this annual event (against Ryan, Grover and Wiswell).

NO. 4 Walter Hallman

Mr. Hallman, who hails from Indiana, was runner-up to Ryan at the 2nd National Tourney in Tacoma and still more recently won the 1944 Indiana Championship. There is little to choose between Messrs Freyer and Hallman. An encounter between these youthful masters might well produce a future contender for World honors.

NO. 5 Basil Case

In 1944 this sensational Dixie Master won the Southern States Championship for the sixth consecutive time. In 1941 he played a twenty game match in Miami against Newell Banks which resulted in twenty draws. Case, who is the idol of the South, is a very studious player with an extensive knowledge of book play. He is a dangerous opponent at all times and will undoubtedly be heard from in future national competitions.

NO. 6 Newell Banks

Mr. Banks is the present World's Champion Blindfold Player and a veteran of many famous encounters. His recent match with Case proves he is still in top form and a player to be reckoned with. His latest achievement was a victory over Wiswell in a twenty game stake match in 1942, sponsored by the city of Miami. Some years back he lost a

world's title match to the late Robert Stewart by the close score of 2 to 1 and 37 draws.

NO. 7   Jesse B. Hanson

Jesse is known as "The Mystery Man of Checkers" and has traveled all over the world in his quest for opponents worthy of his steel. His recent gallant defense of the Pacific Coast Title, which he held against all comers for over a quarter of a century, stamps him as one of America's best, a position he has held for many years. (See Biography for additional data.)

NO. 8   Alex Cameron

For some time Mr. Cameron has been Champion of the state of Florida and has been a high prize winner in many American Championship Tourneys. His latest success was his defeat of the late L. M. Lewis in a forty game match in Miami. On several occasions he was runner-up to Case in the Southern States Tourneys. "Alex" is a very careful player and moves only after long and concentrated deliberation.

NO. 9   John B. Stiles

Our No. 9 man tied for third prize at the 2nd National Tourney and has held the Minnesota title no less than seven times. He has also won major prizes in various other national tourneys besides playing and winning matches against some of America's foremost masters. He is a recognized authority on the three move opening and author of numerous guides on this style of play.

NO. 10 Tommie Wiswell

"The Wizard of Gotham," as he is known to the Checker world, played numerous matches and tourneys prior to his entrance into the Army. His last match in civilian life was a thirty game subscription affair against Alex Cameron

which the New Yorker won by five wins to one. He was formerly New York Champion and has an even tourney record
with Harold Freyer.

There you have it! Because they have shown a desire to
retire from active play such famous *stars* as Asa Long, Edwin
F. Hunt, Nathan Rubin, Harry Lieberman, Louis Ginsberg and
several others were not considered in the above rating. In
other words the Committee based their decisions on the recent
match and tourney record of each player.